MW01049077

JOSEY
BAKER
BREAD

JOSEY BAKER BREAD

JOSEY BAKER

PHOTOGRAPHS BY ERIN KUNKEL

CHRONICLE BOOKS

SAN FRANCISCO

Text copyright © 2014 by **Josey Baker.**
Photographs copyright © 2014 by **Erin Kunkel.**
All rights reserved. No part of this book may be reproduced
in any form without written permission from the publisher.

Library of Congress Cataloging-in-Publication Data available.

ISBN 978-1-4521-1368-5

Manufactured in China

Designed by **Vanessa Dina**
Prop styling by **Ethel Brennan**
Typesetting by **Howie Severson**

10 9 8 7 6 5 4 3 2 1

Chronicle Books LLC
680 Second Street
San Francisco, California 94107
www.chroniclebooks.com

This book is dedicated to my mom.
Clear a space on the shelf for this one,
Mama.

CONTENTS

toast!

#1 dark mountain rye
with cream cheese $3.50

#2 whole wheat with $3.75
butter + almond butter

country bread with $3.50

INTRODUCTION:
take my hand

me: Well, hello there! I'm so totally pumped that you and I are here together, sharing this moment. I mean, this is the culmination of a TON of hard work, and I think this is the beginning of something really, really beautiful. . . .

you: Whoaaa there, hold your horses. I don't even know you! I just picked up this book to take a peek, not to have some awkward "very meaningful moment" with a stranger.

me: Oh, I'm sorry. I don't mean to get too excited too quickly—but come on, just take my hand. It'll be fine, I promise.

you: Ummm, okay, I will take your hand . . . who are you anyway??

me: YES! Awesome. I'm Josey, Josey Baker, And yes, that is my real last name. And no, NOT Josie like Josie and the Pussycats. Josey like *The Outlaw Josey Wales.* I'm just a fella who started baking bread at home one day, fell totally in love with it, and decided to turn it into my job.

you: Are you serious? You just decided to start baking bread, and now it's your job? No schooling? No jobs at bakeries? What the heck?

me: Yup, that's how it went down. A buddy of mine was traveling through San Francisco, and he swung by with a sourdough starter, a tiny nugget of which he left with me, along with some scribbled instructions. A few days later I tried it out, and I was smitten. Truth is, I just couldn't stop baking. I baked, and baked, and baked, 'til I had too much bread to eat, too much bread to store in my freezer, even too much bread to give away.

you: Really? What did you do with all this bread?

me: Wait just a second here—I feel like I'm talking too much. I'm very interested to hear about you as well. Why are you reading this book?

you: <insert your own very personal answer here>

me: Super-cool! That is exactly what I'd hoped you would say. I mean, I literally wrote this book for YOU. It's amazing that this is happening right now, don't you think?

you: All right, I'm getting warmed up to this whole thing. . . . So wait, what did you do with all that bread you were baking?

me: I started selling it. And I'll be damned, people started buying it! I started out baking one loaf at a time, then two, then four, until eventually I was baking twelve loaves at once in my dinky little home oven. I'd get up at 3 A.M. to start baking, squeezing in little naps while the bread baked. Then I'd go to work all day (I might have spent a moment here and there watching YouTube videos about bread, just maybe), come home, and stay up 'til midnight lugging tubs of dough up and down stairs, storing it in a used refrigerator in my basement. I did this early in the morning and late at night, since I had a full-time job with an hour commute (it was only uphill the way there). But it was funny—I almost didn't have a say in the matter, and the mission was always clear: Figure out how to make the bread better and how to make more of it.

you: I love it when that happens. When you just want to spend all of your time doing something, and then you can figure out a way to do it—that's really nice. And very rare. Do you know how lucky you are?

me: I do, I do! I feel super-lucky, and fully PUMPED UP. And now bread baking is my job! I bake every single loaf of bread real nice, so that my buddies and

neighbors have some good food to share with their buddies and neighbors.

you: I like the sound of that. But what is this book all about? It's not just about how you fell in love with bread and turned it into your job, right? I mean, this is a cookbook, isn't it?

me: Aha, you are a very curious reader, aren't you? Of course it's a cookbook! I'm gonna tell you how I learned to bake bread, but I'm also gonna teach you how to bake bread yourself, and a bunch of other stuff, too. There are eight chapters, each one sharing a tidbit of my tale and teaching you how to bake a different type of baked good, mostly bread. The beginning of the book focuses on teaching you to make a delicious, crunchy-crusted, wonderfully moist loaf of bread. This is where my bread-baking journey began, and I suggest you do the same. After you've got this under your belt, you'll find a bunch of other super-delicious recipes, including Seed Feast, 100 Percent Whole Wheat, the Raddest Homemade Pizza the World has Ever Known, Dark Mountain Rye, maple walnut scones, and chocolate chip cookies made with brown butter, to name just a few.

you: Sounds great. So that's it, huh? I just follow your recipes, bake some incredible stuff, and have a nice day?

me: Kind of. I mean, anyone can look up a standard bread recipe and follow it. But if you actually want to learn to bake great bread, bread that will make your friends think you have magical powers, you've gotta focus on one thing and improve it until it's totally awesome. That's what we're going to do, you and me. The recipes in the first few chapters are graduated, with each one building on what you did and learned in the last one. We decided to call these graduated recipes "lessons." We start out nice and simple, and each lesson gets a little more nuanced, a little more complicated, a little more delicious. So allow me to hold your hand, from beginning to end—just read the book and bake some bread along the way. If you're already an experienced baker, do me a favor and still start reading at the beginning. You can start baking whenever the spirit moves you. Or you can ignore everything I just said and do what you want.

you: Ignoring you sounds pretty good to me. . . . This is exciting!

me: YES! Let's do it! As my friend Denyse likes to say, "Let's get drunk and shoot stuff."

you: I'm not sure about that, but I AM ready to bake some bread.

where's the equipment section?

There isn't one. Most cookbooks start off with a lengthy explanation of all the tools you need, an overview of the baking process, blah blah blah. When I was first learning to bake, these sections always turned me off. All of that information is helpful, for sure, I just don't think it should be the very first thing you see when you open a cookbook. So I've sprinkled it throughout the book, hopefully at just the time that you're wondering about it. But if you're wondering about something in particular, just look it up in the index, and you'll find the page where you can learn more about it. And if it's not there, use the Internet, or better yet, talk to a baker buddy. And if you don't have one, now's the time to make one. Don't worry, bakers are a generous bunch.

Some very good questions you'll find answers to:

Are there big differences between different types of flour?
(page 19)

What type of loaf pan should I use?
(page 21)

What's the difference between weight and volume in baking? (page 29)

Why not just bake the loaf in a Dutch oven?
(page 34)

What do I use to slash the tops of my loaves? (see page 38)

CHAPTER 1

HOW I FELL IN LOVE / BECAME OBSESSED WITH BREAD / YOUR FIRST LOAVES

"Howdy, ol' boy! I've just spent the last three weeks hiking around some woods, and I think I'll be moseying your way in a few. Ya still got that comfy couch of yours? Mind if I spend a few nights on it?"

George was a buddy from my childhood in Vermont. A few days after the above inquiry he showed up, as he always did, with a backpack towering a foot above his head, tin cups and instruments strapped all over, and a smile from ear to ear.

We were chatting in my kitchen over some tea (maybe some whiskey, too) when I noticed that he had a little jar with a brown lump of clay in it. I asked him what in the heck he was doing carrying that around. He told me that it was sourdough starter, which he'd gotten from a local bakery. I asked, "Why'd you bother to get that stuff? Can you even make decent bread in a home oven?" He chuckled, and proceeded to scribble down some ridiculously simple instructions for making a loaf of sourdough bread.

I'd never baked bread before, and until I saw this simple recipe, I'd always thought of bread as something mystical, the making of which was out of the reach of mere mortal men and women. *I mean, don't bakers have hyper-sophisticated equipment and skills that can be employed only in the dark of night, their magical powers having been passed down from generation to generation? And bread has living things in it, right? How am I supposed to manage that? And it takes, like, hours, if not days,* *to make?* You'll have to excuse me, but ef that. I'll gladly hand over a few bucks for someone else to go through the trouble.

George came and went, but a little lump of his sourdough starter found a home on my kitchen shelf, and his recipe got stuck on my fridge. I glanced at the recipe every morning over a bowl of oatmeal, and eyed the starter every evening over a beer (or cup of tea). After a week of this, I decided my time had come. I read and reread the instructions, never having attempted to make a loaf of sourdough bread before. I rolled up my sleeves and covered the kitchen in flour. Aside from a few minutes spent mixing and kneading, mostly what I did was wait. It was actually kind of boring. I didn't really think it was gonna work, but I figured I'd follow through and bake it, just to see what happened.

And when I bit into that loaf, I couldn't frikkin' believe it: The bread tasted incredible. It wasn't perfect by any means, but that flavor. . . .The fact that this loaf of bread was actually good, that it hadn't turned into some inedible burnt brick, gave me confidence that I had what it takes to bake bread. Little did I know I had unleashed a bread-baking beast whose appetite would lead to some unforeseen problems.

I hope that these first few recipes do the same for you. Just let that bread-baking beast out. You know you want to.

HEY, what's the deal with the first few recipes?

If you go ahead and bake the first several loaves in this book, you might find yourself thinking, "Ummm, these are kinda similar. What is this guy thinking?" So here I am to tell you, before you start asking any awkward questions.

The first handful of recipes—we're calling them lessons—in this book are intertwined and build on one another. The first lesson is the simplest—it has the fewest possible steps and ingredients for a good loaf of bread. It's set up this way to encourage you to just start baking. I purposefully left out a bunch of details, equipment, and ingredients that will help you make even better bread, because I didn't want to overwhelm you if you've never baked before. But if you have baked bread before and are trying to take your bread to the next level, you might want to just read through this first lesson and start your actual baking with a later recipe.

The second lesson builds on what you did and learned in the first recipe. It introduces a second type of flour—whole wheat—and also breaks the mixing of the dough into two separate stages. This recipe will make an even tastier loaf than the first. For the third lesson I teach you how to bake a loaf that requires a little more care, attention, and dexterity. If this is as far as you go on your bread-baking journey, you'll actually already have more tricks up your sleeve than you know. As you'll see in the lessons and recipes after this, you can add all sorts of stuff to this bread and impress that special someone with how versatile a baker you are.

The second chapter is where we start to get into the really good stuff: sourdough bread. I believe wholeheartedly that sourdough bread (and by that I just mean bread made with a sourdough starter, compared to bread made with yeast you buy in a store) is the best kind of bread, for a bunch of reasons: It tastes better, it stays fresh longer, and lots of people say that it's actually better for you. Also, it's more fun—your sourdough starter is a pet that will help you make countless loaves of delicious bread, just as long you remember to feed it with flour and water every once in a while. First I'll teach you how to make your own sourdough starter, then I'll show you how to use your starter to make bread. From there we'll go to all sorts of awesome and delicious places and encounter tasty baked goods such as pizzas, pocketbreads loaded with bacon or peanut butter cups, and the types of recipes that make a casual home baker happy: cookies, scones, and fruit crumbles.

Okay, enough reading, baker. Roll up them sleeves and make it happen.

you can make bread
JUST LIKE THIS,
I promise.

WHAT YOU'LL NEED

FOODSTUFF	TOOLS
bread flour	measuring spoons
sea salt, fine grind	measuring cups
yeast (the kind in little packets, "active dry," is just fine)	big mixing bowl (at least 6 in/15 cm tall and 12 in/31 cm wide)
lukewarm water	plate or plastic wrap (to cover bowl)
	oil or nonstick spray
	loaf pan (about 8 by 4 in/20 by 10 cm)
	aluminum foil
	towel or pot holders
	cooling rack (optional)

YOUR FIRST LOAF OF BREAD

All right y'all, let's get started. Don't be a weenie; you have everything you need to do this. You don't need any fancy anything—just flour, water, yeast, and salt. Basically you mix 'em up, rub 'em around in the bowl, leave for a long time, then shape it into a log and stick it in a hot oven. What do you get? Your first loaf of delicious home-baked bread, that's what.

BE PATIENT, YOUNG BAKER. Read through the entire lesson before you actually do anything. Trust me—it will make the whole thing easier and better.

PLAN AHEAD. Good bread takes time, and there's just no way around it. You spend 10 minutes mix-ing up your bread dough on day one, and then leave the dough in the fridge for a few days before doing anything else. So plan ahead, and invite someone over for dinner *this weekend.*

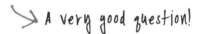 A very good question!

WILL I REALLY BE ABLE TO BAKE GOOD BREAD IN MY HOME OVEN?
Say it with me now, "I AM a baker. I AM a baker. I AM A BAKER." Don't worry, even if your home oven isn't the newest, fanciest oven in the world, chances are it's fully capable of churning out some delicious loaves of bread. For the first couple of recipes you bake the loaves in bread pans, but after that you essentially create an oven inside your oven with a pizza stone and a metal pot or bowl. I've baked in tons of people's home ovens, and I haven't found one that couldn't turn out a perfectly delicious loaf. So don't stress about the oven; just make the bread.

1. **Gather your foodstuff and tools.** Get all the stuff that's listed in the table.

Congratulate yourself, because you're about to bake your first loaf of bread. Maybe treat yourself to a beer or chocolate bar or whatever it is that makes you feel special.

Scrape the top off of your flour pile.

⤳ A very good question!

WHAT IS "BREAD FLOUR"?

Bread flour is very similar to all-purpose flour. In common parlance, you could call both of them "white flour." They're both made from wheat, and they're both made only from the starchy part of the wheat berry, the "endosperm." So what's the difference? The wheat used for bread flour has more protein than wheat used to make all-purpose flour, and dough made with bread flour is a little bit stronger. (Easy enough to remember, right? More protein makes stronger bread dough.) This is great for bread, because we want our bread to stand up tall and proud. Confused? Want to know more? Don't worry; we'll get all covered in flour later.

2. Measure the ingredients and mix them together.
First do the dry ingredients: bread flour, salt, and yeast. When you're measuring the flour, take your bag (or whatever your flour is in), dig into it with your measuring spoon, and "fluff" up the flour a little bit before you scoop it. Then dip your measuring cup in and get enough flour so that it's piled high in your measuring cup. Use the back of a knife to scrape off the flour mound from your cup, leaving you with a smooth, level top. If you have a digital scale and want to weigh ingredients, go for it. Measurements of less than 3 tablespoons are often too small to register on a scale—depending on what you're weighing. One teaspoon of yeast weighs 3 grams, for instance, and ¼ teaspoon of same less than 1 g, which most home scales won't even register. In the case of these small measurements, I couldn't give accurate weights—so scoop away!

bread flour	3½ cups/525 g
sea salt, fine grind	2 tsp/12 g
yeast, active dry	2¼ tsp/7 g

Pour them into the big mixing bowl, and stir them with your hand so they're mixed evenly, and you can't see any lumps of salt or yeast.

Then comes the water. I talk more about water temperature in the next recipe. For now, if you don't want to take the water's temperature, just use water that is lukewarm to the touch.

lukewarm water (about 1²/₃ cups/395 g, 80°F/27°C)

Pour in the water, roll up your sleeve, and mix it all up with your hand. Mush it up real nice, grabbing it and squishing it through your fingers. You just want to get things mixed evenly, so all of the dough looks the same and there isn't any dry flour left. It should be the consistency of a really wet playdough. This'll take only 30 seconds or so.

If you've mushed it up real nice and there is still some dry flour left in the bowl, add another 1 or 2 Tbsp of water and mix it in. If the dough is more

3. Let the magic happen. Cover the bowl with a plate or some plastic wrap so moisture can't sneak out, and leave it alone for about 3 hours at room temperature. By this point the dough should have blown up like a balloon to about twice its size. Now put it in your fridge, and leave it there for at least a day, but anywhere up to a week is fine. (If you're feeling ridiculously impatient, 3 hours is the absolute minimum time it will take for your dough to cool down, and it's much easier to work with when it's cold.) The longer it stays in the fridge (up to a week), the better the flavor will be, as you're giving the yeasts time to create all sorts of delicious flavors in your dough.

↘ A very good question!

ARE THERE BIG DIFFERENCES BETWEEN DIFFERENT TYPES OF FLOUR?

Yup, there are very big differences. Flour is made from all sorts of different stuff, such as wheat, corn, millet, rye, spelt, Kamut, barley . . . and the list continues! For this recipe I suggest you use bread flour, which is made from wheat. Wheat is remarkable in that it's the only grain that, when mixed with water, will form a stretchy dough that can rise tall and proud, if it's treated right. You can make bread out of whatever flour you want, and later on we will get covered in a few different types, but for now simplify your life and stick with bread flour.

liquidy than a really wet playdough, add 1 or 2 Tbsp of flour. See the question that follows before adding too much flour.

↘ A very good question!

THIS DOUGH FEELS SUPER WET. DID I DO SOMETHING WRONG??

Good—it should feel wet! If you've measured everything correctly, the dough should feel like a really wet playdough, or maybe a really dry pancake batter. You won't be able to pour it, but it will want to slouch down in the bowl when you aren't touching it. This dough is definitely a bit wetter than what most beginning bakers are comfortable with, and that is just the way it should be. Don't fret; you don't have to handle the dough very much anyway (you won't be kneading it on a countertop or anything), so the fact that it is so wet won't make things tricky for you. When it comes time to handle the dough again, it will be cold from the fridge and much easier to work with.

4. Shape into a loaf. Oil or spray the inside of your loaf pan, then take your dough out of the fridge. It will be a little sticky, but don't worry—this is the way it should be. Just sprinkle a small handful (about 2 Tbsp) of flour on your countertop and on top of the dough in the bowl. Tip the bowl over, and gently squish the dough out. Sprinkle another little bit (1 Tbsp or so) of flour on top of the dough so it doesn't stick to your hands, and flatten the dough into a circle. Fold the left side of the dough into the center, then fold in the right side, and then gently roll the dough into a log, and plop it into the loaf pan with the smooth side facing up.

Just a lil' bit of flour on top...

then flatten and fold in the sides.

roll it up...

into a delicious little package.

scoop it up...

and plop it in your pan.

make a foil tent.

⤷ A very good question!

WHAT TYPE OF LOAF PAN SHOULD I USE?

This recipe makes about 2 pounds/900 grams of dough, which will fill out a pan that is 8½ by 4½ by 2 in/ 21.5 by 11 by 5 cm. If you have strong feelings about the final shape of your loaf, you'll need to get a pan that matches your vision, but all of the bread recipes in this book assume a loaf pan of dimensions similar to those just listed. I've had great experiences with Chicago Metallic's bakeware, but I am sure there's plenty of other great stuff out there. Search your local kitchen supply store, or look around on the Internet.

5. Let the loaf rise. Spray or brush the top of the loaf with oil (so the foil doesn't stick to it), and then cover the loaf with aluminum foil. Tent the foil so that there's room for the dough to rise about 2 in/5 cm.

Now for the hard part: Leave it alone for about 4 hours. Put it somewhere out of the way so it won't be disturbed, like on top of your fridge or just on a shelf in your kitchen. If you can't bake it in 4 hours, let it sit out for a couple of hours, then put it back in the fridge for anywhere from 1 to 3 days (exact timing doesn't matter here).

6. Bake that baby. If your loaf has been in the fridge, take it out so it can warm to room temperature while the oven preheats. Put one of the racks in your oven to the middle height. Turn on your oven to 475°F/240°C, and let it preheat for at least 20 minutes. Take your loaf, complete with aluminum foil covering, and put it in the oven for 20 minutes. At this point, open up your oven, take off the aluminum foil, and get excited—your dough is turning to bread! Bake for another 20 minutes, and take a look—if the top is a nice dark brown, take it out. If not, leave it in for another 7 or 8 minutes.

7. Let that sucker cool down! For real; you're just gonna burn your mouth if you eat the bread when it's too hot. Use a towel or pot holders to take the bread out of the pan (if it sticks in the pan, use a spatula or butter knife to gently loosen it). Leave the bread on a cooling rack or lean it against something so air can flow around it while it cools. It's best to let it cool for an hour, but I know you. . . . Just wait 30 minutes and eat the whole thing.

➘ A very good question!

WHY ISN'T MY BREAD TURNING OUT THE WAY I WANT IT TO?

Aha, a very good question, ambitious baker that you are. To answer that question, I need to know what's wrong with your bread. Did you measure all of your ingredients correctly? Did you wait the right amount of time for each step? Was the water the right temperature? Everything is connected, so if you change any of the details, it throws the whole thing off. One bit of advice—don't lose hope! You are a bread baker; you just haven't realized it yet. Here are some specific problems with some suggestions:

- **The bread is too dense!** Awww man, I hate it when that happens. This is tricky—it could be happening for a bunch of different reasons. Bottom line: The dough didn't trap the gas made by the yeast, or the yeast didn't make enough of this gas. This might have to do with temperature, so lemme ask—are you making the bread in a place that's a little warm (above 80°F/27°C) or a little cool (below 60°F/15°C)? If it's warm, then it's likely that the bread sat for too long (effectively popping like a balloon), so try letting the dough sit for less time after you've shaped it, maybe 2 hours. If it's a little cool where you are, then perhaps the yeast didn't get a chance to do its thing (didn't create enough gas to make the loaf rise), so try letting it sit a little longer, maybe 6 hours after you've shaped it into a loaf. (For tips on how to know when the loaf is ready to go into the oven, check out page 72.)

- **The bread is burnt!** Oh no. The first thing I wonder about is how hot your oven *actually* is. Ya see, whatever you set your oven dial to is not necessarily what temperature your oven warms up to. If you want to be sure about this, get an oven thermometer and use it. Also, make sure that you bake your bread on the middle rack of the oven—bread can easily burn if it's too near the top or bottom of the oven. Anyway, to avoid this terrible burnt disaster you should try ONE of the following things: Lower the temperature of your oven, down to 450°F/230°C or even 425°F/220°C; bake it for less time (try 35 minutes); or make sure the bread is positioned in the middle of the oven.

- **The bread is gooey!** Ewwww. Did you wait for it to cool? When the bread first comes out of the oven it is actually still baking, so you simply must give it time to cool down. But if you were good and patient, it was probably underbaked. Try ONE of the following: Turn your oven up a little higher (try 500°F/260°C), leave the bread in the oven for another 8 to 10 minutes, or use a little less water in your dough. Once it's nice and dark brown and the house smells delicious, your bread should be fully baked.

oh, baby,
oh, baby:
the dough is becoming bread!

WHAT YOU'LL NEED

FOODSTUFF	TOOLS
yeast (the kind in little packets, "active dry," is just fine)	measuring spoons
	measuring cups
water	thermometer (optional)
whole-wheat flour	big mixing bowl (at least 6 in/15 cm tall and 12 in/31 cm wide)
bread flour	mixing spoon (optional)
sea salt, fine grind	plate or plastic wrap (to cover bowl)
	oil or nonstick spray
	loaf pan (about 8 by 4 in/20 by 10 cm)
	aluminum foil
	cooling rack (optional)

A TWO-PART MIX

How did that first loaf turn out? (You say, "Awesome.") Are you ready for an even better loaf of bread? (You say, "Heck yes, Baker.") Rad—let's do it. This lesson is super-similar to the first, but we use a little bit of whole-wheat flour, and we mix the dough in two stages. First you mix up a little whole-wheat flour, water, and yeast, and let that sit overnight. This is called your "pre-ferment." In the morning you mix in the bread flour, water, and salt and basically do everything the same as with the first loaf. "But why?" you so curiously ponder. By adding a little whole-wheat flour and using a pre-ferment, we're developing a bread with better flavor that will stay fresh longer.

TAKE IT EASY. As you'll see, this lesson includes quantities for up to four loaves of bread. I'd suggest you keep things simple and just make the one- or two-loaf recipes until you're feeling comfortable with the whole thing. Once you're ready for the four-loaf recipe, you'll need to get yourself a larger bowl or maybe even a dough bucket (a 6½-qt/6-L one should be perfect), but don't rush this. You've got plenty of time to make more bread than you can eat. Unless you're baking all of this bread in one go, you'll still only need one or two loaf pans.

1. Gather your foodstuff and tools. Get all the stuff that's listed in the table.

⤳ A very good question!

I AM MIXING UP FLOUR, WATER, AND YEAST, BUT THIS ISN'T MY BREAD DOUGH. WHAT IS IT?

This flour/water/yeast mixture goes by many names, but we will call it a **pre-ferment**. The point is to use a little bit of yeast and let it really work for you. By letting the yeast sit in the flour and water for 8 to 12 hours, you're letting the magical process of fermentation run its course. What is fermentation? It's what makes bread so gosh darn special. The yeasts consume simple sugars and then give off acid, alcohol, and carbon dioxide. Carbon dioxide, a gas, is what makes the bread rise and is what will make this pre-ferment nice and bubbly by the time you get to it in the morning.

---

2. Measure and mix your pre-ferment. One night before you go to bed, measure the following, toss 'em into a big bowl, and stir it up with a spoon (or your hand if you're feelin' frisky). And YES—that is only ONE-QUARTER OF A TEASPOON OF YEAST for one loaf of bread. Just trust me on this.

In goes the water . . .

	1 LOAF	2 LOAVES	4 LOAVES
yeast, active dry	¼ tsp	½ tsp	1 tsp
cool water (60°F/15°C)	½ cup/ 120 g	1 cup/ 240 g	2 cups/ 480 g
whole-wheat flour	¾ cup/ 105 g	1½ cups/ 210 g	3 cups/ 420 g

You just want to get things mixed evenly. It'll be like a thick pancake batter. This'll take only 30 seconds or so.

⤳ A very good question!

I SEE THAT THERE ARE TEMPERATURES LISTED FOR THE WATER. IS IT REALLY THAT IMPORTANT?

When you're just starting out it can be overwhelming to try to keep track of all the different variables involved in bread baking—times, temperatures, weights, volumes . . .

a teeny bit of yeast goes a long way.

then whole-wheat flour.

Mix, mix, mix it up good . . .

'til it looks like this!

AHHH!!! The truth of the matter is all of these things affect the final loaf of bread, even if you don't pay any attention to them. I've tried to write the first few recipes so that you don't have to worry about all this stuff, and you can just ease into making some good, old-fashioned bread. But if you want to want to get deep into this and start really perfecting your baking, then break out that thermometer and start keeping track. (I prefer a digital, waterproof, instant-read thermometer, but anything with a range of 40 to 140°F/5 to 60°C will work just fine.) Heck, go all the way—start a bread journal! And if that sounds like no fun, then don't bother. Just follow the recipe and eat the bread.

3. Let the magic happen. Cover the bowl with a plate or plastic wrap so moisture can't sneak out, and put it in a cool place (about 65°F/18°C is perfect) for 12 to 14 hours (overnight is fine). If you're doing this in a warm place (90°F/32°C or above), shorten this phase to 8 to 10 hours—whatever's convenient.

pre-ferment ready to mix into dough.

Roll up your sleeve, and mush it up real nice, squishing the dough between your fingers. You just want to get things mixed evenly. If there's any dry flour left after you've mixed it up, add 1 to 2 Tbsp of water and mix it in, or add 1 to 2 Tbsp of flour if it feels like pancake batter.

↘ A very good question!

WHAT IS THE DEAL WITH THESE DIFFERENT FLOURS? Whole-wheat flour (the brown flour that you're using in this recipe) is just whole wheat berries that have been ground into powder. Easy enough, right? (In truth it's a bit more complicated, but this is fine for now.) All-purpose flour and bread flour are just whole-wheat flour with some of the good stuff taken out. A wheat berry is a seed, but it's kind of like an egg: an awesome little package that is equipped to burst with life under the right conditions. And a wheat berry has different parts, just as an egg does. There's the outer shell of the wheat berry, which is called the bran. (Of course, you don't eat eggshells, but wheat bran is yummy and nutritious.) Then there's the nutrient-rich nugget—in an egg it's called the yolk, and in a wheat berry it's called the germ. So what's left? The white part. In a wheat berry it's called the endosperm. And in an egg . . . you know. In white flour, the wheat bran and germ are removed after the wheat berries have been ground up, and only the endosperm is left.

4. Mix in the rest of the flour and water. Uncover your bowl of pre-ferment and take a peek. There should be a bunch of bubbles on top, and it should be giving off a pleasant acidic/yeasty/alcoholic aroma. If this isn't the case, then be patient and just leave it alone for another few hours. Then mix in:

	1 LOAF	2 LOAVES	4 LOAVES
lukewarm water (80°F/27°C)	1 cup/ 240 g	2 cups/ 480 g	4 cups/ 960 g
bread flour	2½ cups/ 375 g	5 cups/ 750 g	10 cups/ 1,500 g
sea salt, fine grind	2 tsp/ 12 g	4 tsp/ 24 g	2 Tbsp plus 2 tsp/ 48 g

5. Let the magic happen. Cover the bowl so the moisture can't sneak out, and leave it alone for 3 or 4 hours, then put it in the fridge for at least 3 hours, or up to a week. You want to make the dough cold so that it is easier to shape, but the longer you leave it the better the flavor will be.

6. Shape into a loaf. Oil or spray your loaf pan. Sprinkle bread flour on your counter, and pour the dough onto it. If you're making more than one loaf, cut your dough into equal-size pieces. Sprinkle a little bread flour

you ARE SO STRONG!
But be sweet to the
dough; help it get
strong, too.

on top of the dough and flatten it into a circle, then fold in the sides, gently roll it into a log, and plop it into the pan, smooth-side up.

↳ A very good question!

CAN I ADD SOME STUFF TO THIS RECIPE?
Of course you can (and you will), but as the old gym class adage goes, master your somersaults before you start trying to do a double backflip. A lot of mediocre bread is covered up by the addition of yummy things, such as sugar, butter, cheese, etc. If you really want to add other stuff, be my guest, but I think you should perfect your basic loaf before you go getting all crazy with other ingredients. Just my two cents. Follow your heart.

↳ A very good question!

WHY ARE WE MAKING A RECTANGULAR SANDWICH LOAF? I WANT TO MAKE THOSE SUPER-SEXY ROUND LOAVES I SEE IN BAKERIES.

I love how ambitious you are. Truth be told, I'm just trying to take it slow here. I don't want to freak you out, know what I mean? But don't you worry, we're going to get to that type of loaf soon, I promise you. How soon, you wonder? Super-soon—it's the next recipe!

7. Let the loaf rise. Oil or spray the top of your loaf so that foil won't stick, then tent the aluminum foil over the top (leaving room for the loaf to rise) and leave it alone for 4 to 6 hours, or put it in the fridge for 6 to 24 hours.

8. Bake that baby. Preheat your oven to 475°F/240°C for at least 20 minutes. If you put the dough in the fridge, take it out to let it warm up to room temperature. Then put your loaf in the oven for 20 minutes. Take off the aluminum foil, and bake for another 20 minutes. Check the color of the loaf, and take it out, or bake for another 7 minutes if it's light in color.

9. Let it cool on a cooling rack, then enjoy.

BAKER'S PERCENTAGE

Bread flour	73%
Whole-wheat flour	27%
Water	73%
Yeast	About 0.1%
Salt	2.3%

THE BAKER'S PERCENTAGE

Bakers have a funny system for describing the amounts of various ingredients in a given recipe. I say that it's "funny" because there's one little quirk that makes it tricky to understand at first. Basically, all ingredients in a recipe are described as a percentage of the total weight of the flour. The flour is always described as 100 percent, and all other ingredients are described in relation to this. For instance, say that a recipe had 100 g of flour, 70 g of water, 2 g of salt, and 3 g of yeast. The following would be the baker's percentage for that recipe:

EXAMPLE BAKER'S PERCENTAGE

Bread flour	100%
Water	70%
Salt	2%
Yeast	3%

Simple enough, right? Yes, the total percentage is more than 100 percent, and no, it doesn't make any sense. While it may seem weird at this point in your baking career (and honestly, it probably is unnecessary for now), it is extremely valuable once you start tweaking recipes, increasing quantities, and comparing one recipe with another. Don't worry about the baker's percentage for now, but down the line it'll be a great thing to know.

A very good question!

WHAT'S THE DIFFERENCE BETWEEN WEIGHT AND VOLUME IN BAKING?

The main difference is that weight is way more accurate. Many beginning bakers are intimidated by recipes that call for weighing the ingredients, but hands down, it's a superior method. So if you want to start becoming a master baker, get yourself a nice little digital scale—it'll make a world of difference.

To help you understand how bread baking can fit into your day, here are some possible bread-baking schedules. All of them work equally well—they're just different.

Possible Bread-Baking Schedules (PBBS)

WHAT YOU'RE DOING	PBBS #1: "AFTER DINNER"	PBBS #2: "EARLY BIRD"	PBBS #3: "LUNCH BREAK"
mix pre-ferment (step 2)	after dinner, say 8 P.M.	before you go to work/school, say 8:30 A.M.	during your lunch break, maybe 12:30 P.M.
mix dough (step 4)	before breakfast, say 8:30 A.M.	after dinner, say 8 P.M.	about 10 or 11 P.M.
put dough in fridge (step 5)	between 10 and 11 A.M.	between 10 and 11 P.M.	between 1 and 2 A.M.
shape into loaf (step 6)	whenever you want! (3 hours to 1 week after previous step)		
bake (step 8)	whenever you want! (4 to 6 hours after previous step if at room temperature, 6 to 24 hours after previous step if you put loaf in fridge)		

* I love this part of breadmaking.
Roll up the loaves and put 'em to bed.

Holy moly,
I can't believe
I made this!

WHAT YOU'LL NEED

FOODSTUFF	TOOLS
yeast (the kind in little packets, "active dry," is just fine)	measuring spoons
	measuring cups
water	thermometer (optional)
whole-wheat flour	big mixing bowl (at least 6 in/15 cm tall and 12 in/31 cm wide)
bread flour	mixing spoon (optional)
sea salt, fine grind	plate or plastic wrap (to cover bowl)
rice flour	spatula or bench knife
	proofing basket and cloth (see page 35 for other options)
	baking stone and oven-safe pot or bowl (at least 6 in/15 cm tall and 12 in/31 cm wide) OR a Dutch oven
	parchment paper
	large plate or pizza peel
	double-edged razor blade and handle (see page 38)
	cooling rack (optional)

A HEARTH LOAF

This is a different way of baking the same dough that you just made in the previous lesson. Using loaf pans is a fabulous way to start baking, and if you're looking for rectangular loaves, it's the way to go. But I really love me a hearth loaf. (That just sounds so sexy, doesn't it? Say it out loud: *hearth loaf*. So liberated, so rustic, so pure.) For this recipe, you're going to shape the bread into a loaf and let it rise in a little basket, then you're going to bake it directly on the "hearth," or floor of the oven. In your home oven, a baking stone (or Dutch oven) will act as the hearth. Another exciting and dangerous addition to this recipe: You're going to slash the top of your loaf with a razor blade.

1. Gather your foodstuff and tools. Get all the stuff that's listed in the table.

➤ A very good question!

WHY IS THIS LOAF CALLED A "HEARTH" LOAF?
"Hearth" is the name for the bottom of the oven, or fireplace. In professional bread ovens, the bottoms are made of thick slabs of concrete, so that you can bake the bread right on them. These ovens also have steam injectors, which make the baking chamber fill up with steam at the press of a button. But get this—you don't need all that fancy stuff to make an incredible hearth loaf at home. The way that I suggest you bake this loaf, especially if you're a beginning bread baker, is to just use a baking stone with a metal pot or bowl flipped upside down on top of the bread. The baking stone holds on to heat really well, so that the dough can rise quickly when you first put it in the oven. And the metal pot or bowl traps the moisture that evaporates from the dough, providing a nice, steamy environment for the bread to bake in. If you're feeling crafty and are on a budget, instead of a baking stone you can use unfinished quarry tiles, which should be available at your hardware store. As for the metal pot, you just want something that can (1) fit on top of your loaf, (2) get good and hot, and (3) trap the steam from the bread. Make sure your pot or bowl has a flat top, so that it forms a tight seal on the baking stone. Handles are a plus (provided they can withstand high heat), as they make lifting the pot or bowl very easy. Detailed instructions about all of this are given later.

➤ A very good question!

WHY NOT JUST BAKE THE LOAF IN A DUTCH OVEN? I'VE HEARD OF THAT METHOD.

Baking bread in a Dutch oven is a great way to bake hearth loaves at home, for sure. This method was popularized by Jim Lahey's "no-knead" method, and Chad Robertson's gorgeous book *Tartine Bread*. I'm sure other folks have written about it as well, but it was through these two sources that I realized what a miraculous technique it is. It traps all the steam from the baking bread and also blasts the bread with heat, which contributes to "oven spring"—the rapid increase in volume of the loaf upon entering the oven. Oh yeah—by "Dutch oven" I just mean a large, thick-walled pot (with a lid) that is big enough to hold your bread. Cast iron works great, as does Le Creuset. The only issue with the Dutch oven method is that loading your bread into it can be tricky. I've flopped many a loaf into a 500°F/260°C Dutch oven only to have the bread land lopsided or deflate from the impact of being dropped. That being said, if you don't have a baking stone, a Dutch oven is still a wonderful way to bake a hearth loaf.

2. Make the pre-ferment. Measure the following, toss 'em into a big bowl, and stir it up with a spoon (or your hand if you're feelin' frisky):

	1 LOAF	2 LOAVES	4 LOAVES
yeast	¼ tsp	½ tsp	1 tsp
cool water (60°F/15°C)	½ cup/ 120 g	1 cup/ 240 g	2 cups/ 480 g
whole-wheat flour	¾ cup/ 105 g	1½ cups 210 g	3 cups/ 420 g

You just want to get things mixed evenly. It'll be like a thick pancake batter. This will take only 30 seconds or so.

3. Let the magic happen. Cover the bowl with a plate or plastic wrap—just so the moisture can't sneak out of the bowl—and put it in a cool place (55 to 65°F/13 to 18°C) for about 12 hours (overnight is fine, or during the day while you're at work/playing hooky).

4. Mix the dough. Lift the cover and take a peek. There should be a bunch of bubbles on top, and it should be giving off a nice odor—a little tangy and nutty. If this isn't the case, be patient and leave it alone for another 3 to 4 hours. Then mix in:

	1 LOAF	2 LOAVES	4 LOAVES
lukewarm water (80°F/27°C)	1 cup/ 240 g	2 cups/ 480 g	4 cups/ 960 g
bread flour	2½ cups/ 375 g	5 cups/ 750 g	10 cups/ 1,500 g
sea salt, fine grind	2 tsp/ 12 g	4 tsp/ 24 g	2 Tbsp plus 2 tsp/ 48 g

Roll up your sleeve, and mush it up real nice. You just want to get things mixed evenly—don't bother kneading the dough. If there is flour that won't mix into the dough, toss in another 1 to 2 Tbsp or two of water, or add 1 to 2 Tbsp of flour if the dough's too wet.

5. Let the magic happen. Cover the bowl and let it sit for 3 to 4 hours, then stick it in the fridge. Leave it there for at least 3 hours, or up to a week.

⤳ A very good question!

WHY DO I HAVE TO WAIT FOR THE MAGIC TO HAPPEN?

When making yeasted breads—with store-bought yeast or "wild yeast" (sourdough)—you do lots of waiting. But this waiting is when the magic happens. The little yeasts are slaving away for you, reproducing and consuming nutrients in the flour, and in the process making carbon dioxide, alcohol, and acids. These things are all wonderful for bread, but only in the right amounts. If you don't wait long enough, there won't be enough of the yeast's gas to raise the bread, and you'll end up with a dense loaf. But if you wait too long, you'll end up with a similar result, for a totally different reason: Basically, the yeast will blow up the dough beyond its maximum volume, and it will essentially pop, never to rise again. This is a sad occurrence, and a rite of passage in the life of every bread baker. It will probably ruin your day, but the next day will be brighter, I promise.

Here's where we start to get crazy, compared with what we've been doing thus far. Brace yourself. Take a deep breath. Let's do it.

6. Shape your loaf. Sprinkle a handful of bread flour on your counter, and pour the dough out. If you're making more than one loaf, cut your dough into equal-size pieces. Be nice and gentle with the dough—it has gas in it, and you want to keep most of it there. Gently grab a corner of the dough and fold it up and over into the middle. Do the same thing around the entire piece of dough until you've folded in the dough around the entire perimeter, and you've just got a tight little seam on top. Flip your loaf so that the seam you just made is facing down, using a spatula or bench knife if it sticks at all to the table. Let it sit there for a few minutes, to encourage the seam you just made to stick together.

7. Prepare the proofing basket. Take your proofing cloth (see the following "proofing basket" info) and lay it flat on your counter. Sprinkle a handful of **rice flour** on it, and rub it into the fabric with your fingers. (Rice flour is amazing in that it almost guarantees your dough won't stick to the cloth.) Now tuck the cloth into your proofing basket and adjust it so that there aren't many sharp corners for the dough to get stuck in. Sprinkle the cloth with another 1 Tbsp of rice flour.

⤳ A very good question!

WHAT'S A PROOFING BASKET?

Once you've shaped your dough into a loaf, you let it "proof"—this is just a fancy of way saying that you leave it alone so that the yeast can produce carbon dioxide, thereby making the loaf expand and giving it a nice, airy texture. So now that we know this, you can probably guess what a "proofing basket" is—a basket in which you let your loaf proof! A proofing basket gives support to the dough, so that it can keep its shape while it rises. The loaf stays in the proofing basket right up until it goes in the oven. There are lots of different styles for proofing baskets. They come in a bunch of different materials,

Don't be skimpy with that rice flour.

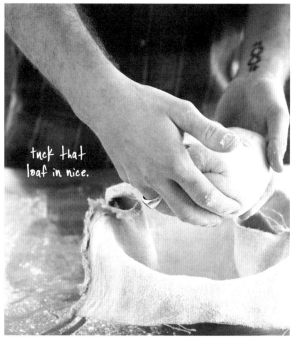

tuck that loaf in nice.

cover the loaf to trap in the steam.

such as willow, wicker, and plastic. And they come in a bunch of different shapes and sizes—round ones, long skinny ones, short fat ones, and everything in between.

For YOUR proofing basket you can use any number of things: a colander, a wicker basket, or even just a mixing bowl. It's best if the basket has holes in it, but a bowl will work just fine. Use a piece of fabric that is tightly woven, such as linen or a cotton napkin. Just don't use a towel that has little "barbs" on it, or else your loaf may stick when you're about to bake it, and that will totally screw up your day. Using rice flour on your proofing cloth will really help your loaf not stick to it.

8. Let your loaf rise. Use your spatula or bench knife to scoop up the shaped loaf, and plop it into the basket, smooth-side down. If you want to bake the bread in 4 to 6 hours, let the loaf sit out somewhere in your kitchen. If you want to bake it anywhere from 6 to 24 hours later, stick the loaf in the fridge (or just outside if it's cool out—about 45°F/7°C).

9. Preheat your oven. Once your loaf has risen, put your baking stone or Dutch oven on the middle rack of your oven and preheat at 475°F/240°C for 30 minutes. Don't skimp on this—you want everything to get good and hot before the bread goes in.

10. Bake your bread. Put a piece of parchment paper on top of your loaf, followed by the large plate or pizza peel (if you have one). Flip the whole thing over so that your loaf comes out of the proofing basket and is sitting on the parchment. (Or carefully plop the loaf into your preheated Dutch oven, omitting the parchment.) Now use the razor blade to slash the top of that loaf with deft speed! (See the pointers on page 38.) Open up your oven, slide the loaf (and parchment) onto the middle of your baking stone, then carefully invert the pot or bowl over the loaf (or put the lid on the Dutch oven). Bake for 20 minutes, then CAREFULLY take the hot pot or bowl off your loaf (or take off the Dutch oven lid), and remove the parchment. Bake for another 15 minutes, and check the bread to see how it's looking. If it's not dark brown, give it another 5 to 10 minutes.

↘ *A very good question!*

WHAT IS PARCHMENT PAPER? DO I HAVE TO USE IT?
Parchment paper helps your bread slide to and fro without sticking to anything. And it's safe to go into the oven, at least for a while, without catching on fire. That being said, you should take out your parchment paper when you uncover your loaf of bread, because there's a good chance that the paper will turn black if you leave it in the whole time. If you don't feel like using parchment paper, or don't have any, you can sprinkle your loaf with cornmeal or bread flour, which will help your loaf slide into the oven.

take out that parchment before it burns.

11. Let it cool, you impatient baker. Take out the bread and put it on a cooling rack or just lean it on its side so that air can move freely around it. Resist the very strong urge to eat it immediately—it's not done baking yet. Have some self-control!

BAKER'S PERCENTAGE

Bread flour	73%
Whole-wheat flour	27%
Water	73%
Yeast	About 0.1%
Salt	2.3%

Some Pointers on Slashing

Slashing your first loaf is probably going to be one of the most exciting moments of your life. It's the culmination of many, many hours of love and care, and it requires every bit of attention you can muster. It's also a great reminder that confidence goes a long way. When it's time to slash that loaf, just act like you know exactly what you're doing. Don't get all nervous that you're going to ruin the bread. You're not going to ruin the bread. You're going to help that loaf become the truest, fullest version of itself. That being said, here are a few things to keep in mind while you are totally showing that loaf who is boss:

- **USE A DOUBLE-EDGED RAZOR BLADE.** These little guys are the best tools for the job. They're thinner and sharper than anything else (including single-edged razor blades), meaning that it's easier to get a smooth cut in your bread dough. To make a little handle for your razor, take a Popsicle stick or wooden coffee stirrer and slip it through the holes like that picture on the facing page. You will have to whittle down your Popsicle stick.

- **START SIMPLE.** There are a million different ways to slash a loaf of bread, but let's take it easy. Start with a single slash down the middle of the loaf. This is the easiest to get right, and it will let the loaf get nice and big, even if you're a little sloppy.

- **GO FAST.** Lots of beginners get squeamish and drag the blade across the dough too slowly, perhaps worried that they're going to hurt the bread. Not only does the bread understand, but it *wants* to be cut. So don't ef around, just cut the bread, and cut it quick.

- **CUT ABOUT ¼ IN/6 MM DEEP.** Don't worry about hitting exactly ¼ in/6 mm in depth, but shoot for right around there. If you go too deep or too shallow, the cut won't tear open and get sexy the way it wants to.

- **ANGLE THE BLADE.** By holding the blade at somewhere around a 45-degree angle to the dough, you're encouraging the cut to tear open and form an "ear." Everybody's different, but I think this is the sexiest thing that can happen on top of a loaf of bread.

- **CUT WITH A (SLIGHT) CURVE.** If your slash has a mild arc to it, this too will encourage the dough to rip open and form an ear. Don't go overboard here; the slightest of curves will do wonders for your slash.

MANY LOAVES IN ONE

You are actually in a very powerful place, young baker. Even though you've only been improving a single type of bread, you actually know how to bake many different types! Here's the thing—you can take this simple loaf of bread and add all sorts of stuff to it, thereby creating many different breads.

Let me be clear—*the following recipes are almost exactly the same as the previous recipe. All you do is add some new yummy stuff when you mix up your dough.*

Some additives (such as seeds) soak up water from the dough, while others (such as olives) add water to the dough, and others (such as cheese) don't really do anything. We take this into account by letting thirsty additives like seeds soak in water before adding them to the dough. It's no big deal either way—remember that you're just baking bread. Here are a few ideas for adding goodies to your loaves, but don't stop there— you can add whatever you want. (Seriously. I've added stuff like cereal and chocolate peanut butter cups, and they've made delicious loaves of bread. Get wild.)

WHAT YOU'LL NEED

FOODSTUFF	TOOLS
sesame seeds, brown, unhulled	measuring cups
water	measuring spoons
yeast (the kind in little packets, "active dry," is just fine)	small bowl or jar
	thermometer (optional)
whole-wheat flour	big mixing bowl (at least 6 in/15 cm tall and 12 in/31 cm wide)
bread flour	
sea salt, fine grind	mixing spoon
cornmeal (optional)	2 plates
	plastic wrap (optional)
	small towel (at least 6 by 8 in/15 by 20 cm)
	spatula or bench knife
	proofing basket and cloth
	baking stone and oven-safe pot or bowl (at least 6 in/15 cm tall and 12 in/31 cm wide) OR a Dutch oven
	parchment paper (optional)
	large plate or pizza peel
	double-edged razor blade and handle
	cooling rack (optional)

SESAME

I *looove* the flavor and texture that sesame seeds bring to this loaf. They're a little thirsty, so you've gotta let them soak in some water before adding them to your dough. Covering the outside of your loaf with sesame seeds will have all your friends swooning, for sure. I prefer this as a hearth loaf, but it makes a mean sandwich loaf as well, so follow your heart on that one.

Just so ya know, you'll need about 1⅓ **cups/ 120 g of sesame seeds** per loaf, to fill the inside and coat the outside.

1. Gather your foodstuff and tools.

2. Toast the seeds. Preheat the oven to 350°F/180°C. Spread the sesame seeds on a baking sheet and bake for 10 to 15 minutes, until they're golden-brown and smell yummy.

What an excellent way
to start the day!

3. Make the seed soaker. Measure and mix in a small bowl or jar:

	1 LOAF	2 LOAVES	4 LOAVES
toasted sesame seeds	1/3 cup/ 55 g	2/3 cup/ 110 g	1 1/3 cups/ 220 g
warm water (100°F/38°C)	1/4 cup/ 60 g	1/2 cup/ 120 g	1 cup/ 240 g

Everything else is the same as last time, up until the loaf shaping.

4. Make the pre-ferment. Measure and mix:

	1 LOAF	2 LOAVES	4 LOAVES
yeast	1/4 tsp	1/2 tsp	1 tsp
cool water (60°F/15°C)	1/2 cup/ 120 g	1 cup/ 240 g	2 cups/ 480 g
whole-wheat flour	3/4 cup/ 105 g	1 1/2 cups/ 210 g	3 cups/ 420 g

5. Let it ferment. Cover both bowls with a plate or plastic wrap, and put them a cool place (55 to 65°F/ 13 to 18°C) for about 12 hours.

6. Mix the dough. Mix into your pre-ferment:

	1 LOAF	2 LOAVES	4 LOAVES
lukewarm water (80°F/27°C)	1 cup/ 240 g	2 cups/ 480 g	4 cups/ 960 g
bread flour	2 1/2 cups/ 375 g	5 cups/ 750 g	10 cups/ 1,500 g
sea salt, fine grind	2 tsp/ 12 g	4 tsp/ 24 g	2 Tbsp plus 2 tsp/ 48 g
seed soaker	all of it	all of it	all of it

7. Let the magic happen. Cover the bowl until the dough is doubled in size. (Remember: Rise at room temperature for 3 hours, then in the fridge for at least 3 hours or up to 4 days.)

8. Shape your loaf. Flour your counter and pour the dough out. Gently fold a corner up and over into the middle, and repeat around the entire piece of dough. Flip your loaf so that it's seam-side down.

9. Cover your loaf in seeds. Wet a small towel, gently wring it out, and spread it out on a plate. Spread 1 cup/ 165 g of the sesame seeds on the second plate. Gently lift your loaf and roll it in the wet towel to dampen. Carefully roll your wet loaf in the seeds, getting it completely covered.

Do everything else the same as always!

10. Let your loaf rise. Don't flour the proofing cloth! The seeds will stop the loaf from sticking. Plop your loaf into the cloth-lined basket, seam-side up. Let it rise until it's about 150 percent of its original volume—2 to 4 hours at room temperature, or up to 2 days in the fridge.

11. Preheat your oven. Once your loaf has risen, put your baking stone or Dutch oven on the middle rack of your oven and preheat at 475°F/240°C for 45 minutes.

12. Bake your bread. Sprinkle the loaf with cornmeal (or cover with parchment paper) and invert the proofing basket onto the large plate or pizza peel. (Or carefully plop the loaf into your preheated Dutch oven, omitting the parchment.) Slash the top with the razor, get it into the oven, and cover it with a pot or bowl (or put the lid on the Dutch oven). Bake for 20 minutes, uncover, and remove the parchment. Bake for another 15 minutes, and check the bread to see how it's looking. If it's not dark brown, give it another 5 to 10 minutes.

13. Then let it cool. Take it out of the oven and place it on a cooling rack, or lean it on its side so the air can move freely around it.

FOODSTUFF	TOOLS
yeast (the kind in little packets, "active dry," is just fine)	measuring spoons
	measuring cups
water	thermometer (optional)
whole-wheat flour	big mixing bowl (at least 6 in/15 cm tall and 12 in/31 cm wide)
pitted kalamata olives	
lemons (for zesting)	mixing spoon
fresh rosemary	plate or plastic wrap (to cover bowl)
bread flour	sharp knife
sea salt, fine grind	zester
rice flour	proofing basket and cloth
cornmeal (optional)	spatula or bench knife
	baking stone and oven-safe pot or bowl (at least 6 in/15 cm tall and 12 in/31 cm wide) OR a Dutch oven
	parchment paper (optional)
	large plate or pizza peel
	double-edged razor blade and handle
	cooling rack (optional)

OLIVE

If only I had a quarter for every time I heard someone say, "Oh my god, olive bread is my favorite!" Olive bread seems to really strike a chord with folks, and this is the best recipe I've ever found. It's inspired by the world-renowned Tartine Bakery, here in San Francisco. They like to use an herb mixture (herbes de Provence), while I just opt for good, old-fashioned rosemary. Do what you will; the olives and lemon zest, together with whatever herbs you choose, will get you invited to every dinner party in town.

Just so ya know, for up to 2 loaves, 1 lemon will do, but for 4 loaves you'll need 2 lemons.

1. Gather your foodstuff and tools.

2. Make the pre-ferment. Measure and mix:

	1 LOAF	2 LOAVES	4 LOAVES
yeast	¼ tsp	½ tsp	1 tsp
cool water (60°F/15°C)	½ cup/ 120 g	1 cup/ 240 g	2 cups/ 480 g
whole-wheat flour	¾ cup/ 105 g	1½ cups/ 210 g	3 cups/ 420 g

3. Let it ferment. Cover the bowl with a plate or plastic wrap, and put it in a cool place (55 to 65°F/13 to 18°C) for about 12 hours.

4. Prepare the olives, lemon zest, and rosemary. I like to use kalamata olives, but you can use whatever kind you like, so long as they don't have pits in them. About ⅓ cup/45 g will do for one loaf of bread. Coarsely chop the olives with a sharp knife. Use a zester to get the zest of about half of a medium-sized lemon; you should have about ½ tsp, firmly packed, for each loaf. Mince some fresh rosemary.

5. Mix the dough. Mix into your pre-ferment:

	1 LOAF	2 LOAVES	4 LOAVES
lukewarm water (80°F/27°C)	1 cup/ 240 g	2 cups/ 480 g	4 cups/ 960 g
bread flour	2½ cups/ 375 g	5 cups/ 750 g	10 cups/ 1,500 g
sea salt, fine grind	2 tsp/ 12 g	4 tsp/ 24 g	2 Tbsp plus 2 tsp/ 48 g
olives, coarsely chopped	⅓ cup/ 45 g	⅔ cup/ 90 g	1⅓ cups/ 180 g
lemon zest	½ tsp, firmly packed	1 tsp, firmly packed	2 tsp, firmly packed
fresh rosemary, minced	1 tsp	2 tsp	4 tsp

6. Let the magic happen. Cover the bowl and let it sit until the dough has about doubled in volume. Rise at room temperature for 3 hours, then in the fridge for at least 3 hours or up to 4 days.

7. Shape your loaf. After the dough has completed its bulk rise, flour your counter and pour the dough out. Gently fold a corner up and over into the middle, and repeat around the entire piece of dough. Flip your loaf so that it's seam-side down while you prepare your proofing basket. Dust your proofing cloth with rice flour, line the proofing basket with the cloth, and use a spatula or bench knife to plop the loaf into the basket, seam-side up.

8. Let your loaf rise. Do what's convenient for you, either letting the loaf sit out on the counter or sticking it in the fridge.

9. Preheat your oven. Once your loaf has risen, put your baking stone or Dutch oven on the middle rack of your oven and preheat at 475°F/240°C for 45 minutes.

10. Bake your bread. Sprinkle the loaf with cornmeal or cover with parchment paper, and invert the proofing basket onto the large plate or pizza peel. (Or carefully plop the loaf into your preheated Dutch oven, omitting the parchment.) Slash the top with the razor, get it into the oven, and cover it with a pot or bowl (or put the lid on the Dutch oven). Bake for 20 minutes, uncover, and remove the parchment. Bake for another 15 minutes, and check the bread to see how it's looking. If it's not dark brown, give it another 5 to 10 minutes.

11. Once it's done, let it cool on a cooling rack, or lean it against something so the air can move around it. Then surprise your neighbor with your new, hot loaf.

WHAT YOU'LL NEED

FOODSTUFF	TOOLS
raisins (whatever kind you like!)	measuring cups
water	measuring spoons
yeast (the kind in little packets, "active dry," is just fine)	small bowl or jar
	thermometer (optional)
whole-wheat flour	big mixing bowl (at least 6 in/15 cm tall and 12 in/31 cm wide)
bread flour	
sea salt, fine grind	mixing spoon
cinnamon, ground	2 plates or plastic wrap (to cover bowls)
	oil or nonstick spray
	loaf pan (about 8 by 4 in/20 by 10 cm)
	aluminum foil
	towel or pot holders
	cooling rack (optional)

CINNAMON RAISIN

Who doesn't like cinnamon raisin toast? Jerks, that's who. I'm kidding, but really, cinnamon raisin bread is so gosh darn delicious, especially when it's toasted up real nice, with some melted salty butter on top. This is about as pure a cinnamon raisin loaf as you can get—no added sugar or fat here, just flour, water, salt, cinnamon, and raisins. I like to do this one as a sandwich loaf, but you can go hearth loaf style, if that suits your fancy. Raisins are thirsty, so you've gotta take this into account and let them soak in water for a while before adding them to your dough, then drain them of the pesky water that didn't feel like getting soaked up.

1. Gather your foodstuff and tools.

2. Make the raisin soaker. Measure and mix in a small bowl or jar:

	1 LOAF	2 LOAVES	4 LOAVES
raisins	½ cup/ 70 g	1 cup/ 140 g	2 cups/ 280 g
warm water (100°F/38°C)	½ cup/ 120 g	1 cup/ 240 g	2 cups/ 480 g

Everything else is the same as last time.

3. Make the pre-ferment. Measure and mix:

	1 LOAF	2 LOAVES	4 LOAVES
yeast	¼ tsp	½ tsp	1 tsp
cool water (60°F/15°C)	½ cup/ 120 g	1 cup/ 240 g	2 cups/ 480 g
whole-wheat flour	¾ cup/ 105 g	1½ cups/ 210 g	3 cups/ 420 g

4. Let it ferment. Cover both bowls, and put them in a cool place (55 to 65°F/13 to 18°C) for about 12 hours.

5. Drain the raisin soaker. Pour off the excess water from your raisin soaker.

6. Mix the dough. Mix into your pre-ferment:

	1 LOAF	2 LOAVES	4 LOAVES
lukewarm water (80°F/27°C)	1 cup/ 240 g	2 cups/ 480 g	4 cups/ 960 g
bread flour	2½ cups/ 375 g	5 cups/ 750 g	10 cups/ 1,500 g
sea salt, fine grind	2 tsp/ 12 g	4 tsp/ 24 g	2 Tbsp plus 2 tsp/ 48 g
cinnamon, ground	2 tsp	4 tsp	2 Tbsp plus 2 tsp
raisins, drained	all of them	all of them	all of them

7. Let the magic happen. Cover the bowl and let it sit until the dough has doubled in volume.

8. Shape your loaf. Oil or spray your loaf pan. Sprinkle flour on your counter, and pour the dough onto it. Sprinkle a little flour on top of the dough, gently roll it into a log, and plop it into the pan, seam-side down. Oil the top and cover with aluminum foil, making sure there's room for the loaf to rise.

9. Let your loaf rise. Do what's convenient for you, either leaving it on your counter or putting it in your fridge.

10. Preheat your oven. Once your loaf has risen, put a rack at the middle height in your oven, and preheat at 475°F/240°C for 45 minutes. Take the loaf out of the fridge while the oven is preheating. (If you're making a hearth loaf, you can leave it in the fridge until it's time to bake.)

11. Bake your bread. Slide that loaf into the hot oven, and bake for 20 minutes, then carefully remove the aluminum. Bake for another 15 minutes, and check the bread to see how it's looking. If it's not dark brown, give it another 7 minutes.

12. Let it cool. Use a towel or pot holders to take the bread out of the pan (if it sticks in the pan, use a spatula or butter knife to gently loosen it). Leave the bread on a cooling rack or lean it against something so air can flow around it while it cools. It's best to let it cool for an hour or more before eating it.

[Bread dough likes to relax,
just like you, so don't go
rushing it, you hear?]

CHAPTER 2

TAMING THE WILD YEAST / SOURDOUGH

Prior to unlocking the bread-baking beast inside me, I was actually on the hunt for a new hobby, and I had pretty specific guidelines. I wanted to find something that I could do at home, that was physical, and ideally that I could share with other people. I'd tried my hand at a couple of fermented foods, like kombucha (fermented tea) and kefir (cultured milk, kinda like yogurt but more liquidy), but neither of them really tugged at my heartstrings. But bread—there was something elemental about the whole thing that I found deeply satisfying. And come on, I mean, my last name is BAKER. You've gotta be kidding me.

Bread dough usually has yeast in it, and that yeast is either bought from a store or cultivated in a "sourdough starter." I'd never baked bread with yeast from the store, but that was fine by me, because now I had this new pet, my own sourdough starter.

What is going on? How is this stuff going to turn into a sourdough starter?

You're essentially creating a little zoo here—a zoo of wild yeast and bacteria. These microorganisms are already alive on the flour (and on your hands, in your kitchen, and on the breezes as well), and you're just coaxing the populations into the right balance for making bread. You have to throw out part of your starter because lots of these little creatures die valiantly for your cause, and also eat up all the available nutrients in the flour. In the process, they also produce a bunch of acid and alcohol, which is great in small amounts, but too much is not good for your bread.

To keep a sourdough starter alive and healthy, you have to feed it with flour and water every couple of days. And each time you feed it, you throw away most of the starter, leaving behind just a little bit to propagate the culture of wild yeast and bacteria. But it really pained me to throw it away. So I baked with it. After a few weeks of this, the amount of bread I was baking far outweighed the amount of bread I and my roommates could eat. So I started storing it in the freezer. After a few weeks of freezer bread my roommate, Brendan, confronted me: "Dude, you can't put any more bread in the freezer."

"But, why not? I mean, where am I supposed to put it?"

"I don't know . . . give it away to people? Just don't put it in the freezer—we don't have room for anything else in there. What are you saving all the bread for, anyway?"

Good question. But give it away? Okay, I can try that. From the very beginning of my love affair with bread I'd been sharing it, bringing it to parties and such, but I hadn't yet warmed up to the idea of just *giving it away*. But heck, I had to do something—I had to keep baking, and there really wasn't anywhere to put the bread.

I gave bread away for a few weeks, dropping off loaves to my neighbors and coworkers. They were always super-appreciative of the gift. And then one day my neighbor Michael said, upon receiving a loaf, "Here, let me give you a few bucks for this."

"No, no, no, dude, I don't want any money . . . okay, five bucks would be fine."

Wait a second—why don't I just start selling the bread? Making money was an afterthought; what I really wanted to do was support my baking habit. And if I made a little cash on the side, what the heck? I wasn't greedy for cash, but I also wasn't turning it away.

So sell my bread I did—first to my friends and coworkers, then to strangers out of my friend's shop, Gravel & Gold, and also out of the bar where I worked, Amnesia.

But soon people started asking for my bread, expecting my bread, e-mailing me about my bread. I had a full-time job. I was baking out of my home oven. My roommates were getting tired of bread crumbs all over our kitchen floor. This could only get so big.

Holy crap, how did this happen?!? I'm a baker? This is totally awesome. Ambitious fellow that I am, I thought, let's see just how big this whole bread thing can get.

In this chapter you'll learn how to make your own sourdough starter and use it to make some bread. Now let's see how big YOUR bread thing can get.

WHAT YOU'LL NEED

FOODSTUFF	TOOLS
whole-wheat flour	quart/liter container with a lid (yogurt tub or mason jar)
water	measuring cup
	mixing spoon

MAKE A SOURDOUGH STARTER

Okay, now we're ready to party. For this recipe you make your own "sourdough starter." PLEASE NOTE: People think sourdough starters are very hard to make or keep alive, and this is most definitely NOT TRUE. On the contrary, sourdough starters are very hard to kill. They're hearty, and mostly what you have to do is leave them alone, mix in a little flour and water now and then, and just believe in them.

1. Mix and ignore. Mix together in an appropriate container:

whole-wheat flour	½ cup/70 g
cool water (60°F/15°C)	½ cup/120 g

Stir it up real good with a spoon. You want it to be the consistency of a thick pancake batter, so add a little more flour or water if it needs it. But don't worry too much about it; exact measurements aren't important here. Loosely cover the container with its lid and let it sit for about 2 days at room temperature (60 to 70°F/ 15 to 21°C).

2. Compost (most of) it. After 2 days, compost most of the starter. Leave about a tablespoon's worth in the container.

3. Feed your starter. Pour in:

cool water (60°F/15°C)	½ cup/120 g

Use a spoon to stir and dissolve the starter that's left in the container. Add:

whole-wheat flour	½ cup/70 g

Stir it up real good, loosely cover, and ignore it for 2 days at room temperature.

4. Repeat. There'll be 2 weeks of this—every 2 or 3 days compost most of your starter and mix in roughly equal parts whole-wheat flour and water. After 2 weeks you'll have a healthy sourdough starter. Now go bake some bread.

WHAT YOU'LL NEED

FOODSTUFF	TOOLS
sourdough starter	measuring cup
water	mixing spoon
whole-wheat flour	

KEEPING YOUR SOURDOUGH STARTER ALIVE AND HEALTHY

If you want to bake only once in a while (once every couple of weeks or less), your starter can live in the fridge.

1. Feed your starter. Every few weeks take it out of the fridge and throw out most of it—compost that stuff. Leave roughly a tablespoon's worth of starter in the container and add:

| cool water (60°F/15°C) | ½ cup/120 g |
| whole-wheat flour | ¾ cup/105 g |

2. Let it warm up, then put it back in the fridge. Stir it up! This will be a little thicker than when you were first making your sourdough starter. Let it sit out for a few hours so the wild yeast and bacteria can do their thing for a little while. Then stick it back in the fridge.

3. Repeat. Just do this every few weeks and your starter can live forever. A few days before you want to bake, take your starter out of the fridge and follow the feeding schedule at right for several days, to get the starter happy and healthy.

If you bake a couple times a week or more, let your starter live on a shelf in your kitchen.

1. Feed your starter. Every couple of days, throw out most of your starter. Leave a tablespoon's worth of starter in the container, and add:

| cool water (60°F/15°C) | ½ cup/120 g |
| whole-wheat flour | ¾ cup/105 g |

Stir it up, and forget about it 'til tomorrow.

2. Repeat. Do this every couple of days and your starter will be healthy and happy and ready to bake whenever you want.

WHAT YOU'LL NEED

FOODSTUFF	TOOLS
sourdough starter	measuring spoons
water	measuring cups
whole-wheat flour	thermometer (optional)
bread flour	big mixing bowl
sea salt, fine grind	mixing spoon
	plate or plastic wrap (to cover bowl)
	oil or nonstick spray
	loaf pan (about 8 by 4 in/20 by 10 cm)
	aluminum foil
	cooling rack (optional)

YOUR FIRST SOURDOUGH LOAF

This is the loaf of bread that I fell in love with. It's a pure and simple loaf, and if done right, it's one of the best. I recommend baking your first sourdough loaf in a loaf pan, but if you're really feeling ready to take on the world, just skip ahead to the next recipe, where we bake a hearth sourdough. Get pumped—everything you've done thus far has been preparation for this loaf. You're gonna pee your pants, it's so good. So go ahead—bake one for you, one for your friend, and one for your mom.

By the way, if you find yourself thinking, "Hmmm, this is just like the last recipe, only instead of making a pre-ferment with commercial yeast, I'm making a pre-ferment with my sourdough starter,"

you are absolutely right. All of the ingredients and measurements are EXACTLY THE SAME as for the other loaves. You just use a little sourdough starter instead of commercial yeast. See—you already know how to do this. Do it, baker.

↘ A very good question!

HOW DO I KNOW IF MY STARTER IS READY FOR BREAD MAKING?

You want to use starter that is very alive and active when you make your sourdough pre-ferment. Your starter should be giving off a pretty sharp and sour smell, but in a good way. It should smell the tiniest bit like vinegar and a tad alcoholic, but it should definitely be appetizing. If you let it go for too long, it can start to give off a super-strong odor that verges on gross, which just means that your starter is overripe. Worry not! It will still make delicious bread. If you've been keeping your starter in the fridge, take it out a day or two before you want to bake, and feed it daily to get it healthy. After a few days' feeding, with the starter at room temperature, it should be ready. The starter is usually ready to be made into a pre-ferment 12 to 24 hours after its last feeding, depending mostly on temperature and how sour you want your bread to be.

1. **Gather your foodstuff and tools.**

2. **Make your sourdough pre-ferment.** You're going to use your sourdough **starter** to make a pre-ferment. Use starter that has a strong sour smell (it should smell a little like vinegar and booze), most likely between 12 and 24 hours old. Mix your pre-ferment in the evening, before you go to bed. You want it to be the consistency of thick pancake batter. Put this stuff in a big bowl:

	1 LOAF	2 LOAVES	4 LOAVES
sourdough starter	1 Tbsp/ 15 g	2 Tbsp/ 30 g	¼ cup/ 60 g
cool water (60°F/15°C)	½ cup/ 120 g	1 cup/ 240 g	2 cups/ 480 g
whole-wheat flour	¾ cup/ 105 g	1½ cups/ 210 g	3 cups/ 420 g

Mix it up real good. Cover with a plate or plastic wrap and leave it alone 'til morning. Go to bed and dream of the amazing bread you'll make tomorrow.

3. **Mix the dough.** Uncover the bowl of pre-ferment, and take a big whiff. It should be putting off a pretty strong smell, nice and yummy, maybe a touch sour. If it doesn't, no biggie, but if ya can, wait another couple of hours. Then add:

	1 LOAF	2 LOAVES	4 LOAVES
lukewarm water (80°F/27°C)	1 cup/ 240 g	2 cups/ 480 g	4 cups/ 960 g
bread flour	2½ cups/ 375 g	5 cups/ 750 g	10 cups/ 1,500 g
sea salt, fine grind	2 tsp/ 12 g	4 tsp/ 24 g	2 Tbsp plus 2 tsp/ 48 g

Stir it up with your strong hands 'til it's good and mixed together (30 seconds to a minute will do). Cover with a plate or plastic wrap, and let it sit for 30 minutes to an hour, whatever is convenient. Go for a walk or read a book or talk to a friend.

4. **Knead the dough.** After it sits for a while, the dough is ready to be kneaded. This makes the dough stronger and redistributes the invisible bread wizards (wild yeast and bacteria). Dip your hand in a bowl of water, then reach down into the side of the dough bowl, grab a little bit of it, and pull it up and push it down on top of the dough. Rotate the bowl a little bit and do it again, dipping your hand in water if it starts to stick. Be sweet and gentle yet firm with the dough. Do this to all of the dough; it'll probably take about ten folds. Cover the dough, and let it sit for ½ hour.

↘ A very good question!

THIS ISN'T KNEADING! IT'S WEIRD! WHAT THE HECK? Indeed, this is a little different from what most people think of as kneading—it's more like stretching and folding. Instead of putting the dough on your countertop and using your strong muscles to rub the dough over and over for many minutes, all the while adding flour to keep it from sticking, and just getting all worked up and sweaty, we are going to let time do a lot of the work. But we're also going to help out, just a little bit, from time to time. For this style of kneading you never actually take the dough out of the bowl. It serves the same purpose as countertop kneading: it makes the dough stronger and redistributes the yeast and bacteria. You'll notice a huge change in the dough between the initial mix and the first time you come back to knead it—it will be much more cohesive, and you'll probably think to yourself, "Holy crap, how did that happen???" Magic, that's how.

5. Knead a few more times. After ½ hour, stretch and fold the dough another ten times. Cover the dough, and leave it alone for another ½ hour. Do this another two times, at ½-hour intervals.

6. Let the magic happen. Leave the dough alone for another 2 to 3 hours, **until it has increased in volume by about half.** (Yes, this is less than before, and yes, it will all still work.) Depending on too many things to list here (but look below if you're curious), this process should take anywhere from 2 to 6 hours longer. Or you can also stick the dough in the fridge and get to it when you like. Just keep an eye on the dough, and don't worry—we are going to focus on this phase in a later recipe!

↳ A very good question!

WHAT AFFECTS HOW QUICKLY BREAD DOUGH FERMENTS?

Oh man, now we are really getting into the deep stuff. How quickly bread dough ferments depends on a *whoole* bunch of variables, such as:

- The amount of yeast (store-bought or wild) in your dough—the more yeast there is, the quicker your dough will ferment

- The consistency of your dough—a wetter dough will ferment faster than a drier dough

- How often your dough is stretched and folded

- The temperature of the dough—warmer dough ferments faster than cooler dough

- The type of flour used to make your dough—the more whole-grain flour you use, the quicker your dough will ferment

Don't worry about any of this stuff for now. Just follow my directions and come back to this in a couple of weeks, and marvel at how much simpler it seems.

7. Shape your loaf. After the dough has completed its bulk rise, flour your counter and dump out the dough. Shape it into a loaf and plop it into a greased loaf pan (check out Lesson 2, step 6, if you need a refresher on this). Oil the top of the loaf, and cover with aluminum foil, tenting the foil so that the loaf can rise.

8. Choose your own path. Now you get to choose your own adventure for the **final rise**. Do what is convenient for you here, folks!

If you want to bake bread in 3 or 4 hours, let the loaf sit out somewhere in your kitchen.

If you want to bake bread anywhere from 6 to 24 hours later, stick the loaf in the fridge (or just outside if it's cool out—about 45°F/7°C).

9. Bake that baby. Preheat your oven to 475°F/240°C for 20 minutes. If you put the dough in the fridge, take it out while the oven is preheating so that the dough and loaf pan can warm up to room temperature before you bake. After 20 minutes of preheating, put your loaf in the oven for 20 minutes. Take off the aluminum foil, and bake for another 20 minutes. Check the color of the loaf; and if it's light in color, bake it for another 7 minutes.

10. Let it cool. Eat that sucker. Is it amazing? I really, sincerely, deeply hope so.

WHAT YOU'LL NEED

FOODSTUFF	TOOLS
sourdough starter	measuring spoons
water	measuring cups
whole-wheat flour	thermometer (optional)
bread flour	big mixing bowl
sea salt, fine grind	mixing spoon
rice flour	plate or plastic wrap (to cover bowl)
cornmeal (optional)	proofing basket and cloth
	spatula or bench knife
	baking stone and oven-safe pot or bowl (at least 6 in/15 cm tall and 12 in/31 cm wide) OR a Dutch oven
	parchment paper (optional)
	large plate or pizza peel
	double-edged razor blade and handle
	cooling rack (optional)

A HEARTH SOURDOUGH

Now this is really it—nothing but flour, water, salt, and wild yeast, baked directly on the hearth, all made by your hands. This is the one, my friend. If this is as far as you get, you have come farther than **99 percent of people**. This is what most people envision when they think of "artisan" or "old-world" or "rustic" bread. It's similar to the hearth loaf in Lesson 3. And ya know what's great? You've already done every piece of the puzzle. Here's your chance to put it all together, baker.

1. Gather your foodstuff and tools.

2. Make your sourdough pre-ferment. Use starter that is sour smelling in a good way, most likely between 12 and 24 hours old. Make your pre-ferment 8 to 12 hours before you want to start mixing your dough—likely in the evening before you go to bed or in the morning. You want it to be the consistency of thick pancake batter. Put this stuff in a big bowl:

	1 LOAF	2 LOAVES	4 LOAVES
sourdough starter	1 Tbsp/ 15 g	2 Tbsp/ 30 g	¼ cup/ 60 g
cool water (60°F/15°C)	½ cup/ 120 g	1 cup/ 240 g	2 cups/ 480 g
whole-wheat flour	¾ cup/ 105 g	1½ cups/ 210 g	3 cups/ 420 g

Mix it up real good. Cover the bowl with a plate or plastic wrap, and put it in a cool place (55 to 65°F/13 to 18°C) for about 12 hours.

3. Mix the dough. Uncover the bowl, and take a big whiff. It should be putting off a pretty strong smell, nice and yummy, maybe a touch sour. If it doesn't, no biggie; it should still make awesome bread. Add:

	1 LOAF	2 LOAVES	4 LOAVES
lukewarm water (80°F/27°C)	1 cup/ 240 g	2 cups/ 480 g	4 cups/ 960 g
bread flour	2½ cups/ 375 g	5 cups/ 750 g	10 cups/ 1,500 g
sea salt, fine grind	2 tsp/ 12 g	4 tsp/ 24 g	2 Tbsp plus 2 tsp/ 48 g

Stir it up with your strong hands 'til it's good and mixed together (30 seconds to a minute will do). Cover and let it sit for 30 minutes to an hour, whatever is convenient. Go for a walk or read a book or talk to a friend.

4. Knead the dough. After it sits for a while, the dough is ready to be kneaded. Dip your hand in a bowl of water, then reach down into the side of the dough bowl, grab a little bit of it, and pull it up and push it down on top of the dough. Rotate the bowl a little bit and do it again. Be sweet and gentle yet firm with the dough. Do this to all of the dough; it'll probably take about ten folds. Cover the dough, and let it sit for ½ hour.

5. Knead a few more times. After ½ hour, stretch and fold the dough another ten times. Cover the dough, and leave it alone for another ½ hour or so. Do this another two times, at ½-hour intervals.

6. Let the magic happen. Leave the dough alone until it has increased in size by about half, which will take 3 to 4 hours.

7. Shape your loaf. After the dough has completed its bulk rise, flour your counter and dump out the dough. Shape it into a loaf and leave it on your counter, seam-side down, while you prepare your proofing basket. Dust your proofing basket with rice flour, and use your spatula or bench knife to plop your loaf into the basket, seam-side up.

8. Let your loaf rise. Remember what you learned from the previous recipe—you get to decide when the loaf is ready for baking, based on its volume. About 150 percent of its original size is good. Regardless, do what's convenient for you:

If you want to bake bread in 3 or 4 hours, let the loaf sit out somewhere in your kitchen.

If you want to bake bread anywhere from 6 to 24 hours later, stick the loaf in the fridge (or just outside if it's cool out—about 45°F/7°C).

9. Preheat. Once your loaf has risen, put your baking stone or Dutch oven on the middle rack of your oven and preheat at 475°F/240°C for 45 minutes. Leave your loaf in the fridge until the oven's preheated—loading hearth loaves into the oven is much easier when the dough is cold.

10. Bake your bread. Sprinkle the loaf with cornmeal (or cover with parchment paper), and invert it onto the large plate or pizza peel. (Or carefully plop your loaf into the preheated Dutch oven, omitting the parchment.) Slash the top with the razor, get it into the oven, and cover it with a pot or bowl (or Dutch oven lid). Bake for 20 minutes, uncover, and remove the parchment. Bake for another 15 minutes, and check the bread to see how it's looking. If it's not dark brown, give it another 5 to 10 minutes.

11. Let it cool. After the loaf has been out of the oven for 30 to 40 minutes, get out your finest bread knife, and let the anticipation build. When you're ready, slice right into the middle of the loaf, and be bewildered by the magic work the wild yeast has done. And feel good about yourself. And don't forget to eat the bread.

WHAT YOU'LL NEED

FOODSTUFF	TOOLS
sourdough starter	measuring spoons
water	measuring cups
whole-wheat flour	thermometer (optional)
bread flour	big mixing bowl
sea salt, fine grind	mixing spoon
rice flour	plate or plastic wrap (to cover bowl)
cornmeal (optional)	marker or tape
	proofing basket and cloth
	spatula or bench knife
	baking stone and oven-safe pot or bowl (at least 6 in/15 cm tall and 12 in/31 cm wide) OR a Dutch oven
	parchment paper (optional)
	large plate or pizza peel
	double-edged razor blade and handle
	cooling rack (optional)

HEARTH SOURDOUGH №2

Thus far the recipes have been pretty prescriptive. I say do this, then do this, then do this. I hope it's been working out well, but now you're ready for the next step. I'm going to start explaining certain things that you should *look for*, and then you're going to decide *what* to do. This is the path to becoming a creative baker, a baker who decides for himself or herself what to do and, just as important, *when* to do it. In this recipe you're going to focus on the "bulk rise" and on making sure that the dough has developed the proper amount in this stage. Everything else will be the same as last time. Go get 'em, baker.

For more in-depth instructions on mixing your dough, check out Lesson 6.

1. Gather your foodstuff and tools.

2. Make the pre-ferment. Measure and mix:

	1 LOAF	2 LOAVES	4 LOAVES
sourdough starter	1 Tbsp/ 15 g	2 Tbsp/ 30 g	¼ cup/ 60 g
cool water (60°F/15°C)	½ cup/ 120 g	1 cup/ 240 g	2 cups/ 480 g
whole-wheat flour	¾ cup/ 105 g	1½ cups/ 210 g	3 cups/ 420 g

3. Let it ferment. Cover the bowl with a plate or plastic wrap, and put it in a cool place (55 to 65°F/13 to 18°C) for about 12 hours.

4. Mix the dough. Mix in:

	1 LOAF	2 LOAVES	4 LOAVES
lukewarm water (80°F/27°C)	1 cup/ 240 g	2 cups/ 480 g	4 cups/ 960 g
bread flour	2½ cups/ 375 g	5 cups/ 750 g	10 cups/ 1,500 g
sea salt, fine grind	2 tsp/ 12 g	4 tsp/ 24 g	2 Tbsp plus 2 tsp/ 48 g

Roll up your sleeve, and mush it up real nice. Mark the side of the bowl with a marker or a piece of tape, so that you know the exact height of the dough in the bowl.

5. Knead the dough. After ½ hour, give your dough its first kneading—dip your hand in a bowl of water, then reach down into the side of the dough bowl, grab a little bit of it, and pull it up and push it down on top of the dough. Rotate the bowl a little bit and do it again. Give the dough about ten stretches and folds. Cover the dough, and let sit for ½ hour.

6. Knead a few more times. After ½ hour, stretch and fold the dough another ten times. Cover the dough, and leave it alone for another ½ hour or so. Do this another two times, at 15- to 30-minute intervals.

7. Let the magic happen. Cover the bowl and let it sit for 2 hours, then . . .

8. Check on the volume of dough. One of the best ways to decide if the dough is ready to be shaped into a loaf is by its volume. This tells you how active the yeast has been, and if the bread dough has enough oomph to carry it through the bake. There are a million different opinions on the matter, but let's just agree that *for this sourdough bread, its bulk rise (see the info below) is done when it's grown in size by about half.* A little under is great, but try to not let it go over. How long this will take depends on a lot of things, but I bet it will take between 2 and 10 hours. You can measure its growth more exactly if your bowl has vertical sides, but you can figure it out regardless. When you check the dough, if it hasn't yet grown by half, you should just wait, in order to give the yeast more time to reproduce and make carbon dioxide. If the dough has grown more than this, proceed with deft speed.

A very good question!

WHAT'S HAPPENING TO CHANGE THE VOLUME OF THE DOUGH?

This phase of bread making is known by many names, but we're going to call it the "bulk rise." Down the line you'll likely start making more than one loaf at a time. (Or you may already be doing this, you ambitious baker, you.) Unless you're making different types of bread, all of the dough will sit together for this first period of fermentation. Since it hasn't yet been divided into loaf-size pieces of dough, we call this the "bulk rise." It's also known as the "bulk fermentation" or "first rise." The second time the bread rises, after it's been shaped into a loaf, is known as "proofing" or "second rise" or "final rise." It's up to the baker to decide when one phase is complete and the next phase can begin. In this recipe we're focusing on the bulk rise, and in the next recipe we'll focus on the final rise. You're growing up so fast.

The rest of this recipe is the same as the previous one—you know how to do it.

9. Shape your loaf. Flour your counter and pour the dough out. Gently fold a corner up and over into the middle, and repeat around the entire piece of dough. Flip your loaf so that it's seam-side down. Rub rice flour into your proofing cloth, line your proofing basket with the cloth, and use your spatula or bench knife to plop your loaf into the basket, seam-side up.

10. Let your loaf rise. Do what's convenient for you: If you want to bake bread in about 3 hours, let the loaf sit out somewhere in your kitchen. If you want to bake bread anywhere from 6 to 24 hours later, stick the loaf in the fridge (or just outside if it's cool out—about 45°F/7°C).

11. Preheat. Once your loaf has risen, put your baking stone or Dutch oven on the middle rack of your oven and preheat at 475°F/240°C for 30 minutes.

12. Bake your bread. Sprinkle 1 tsp or so of cornmeal on your loaf (or put a piece of parchment paper on it) followed by the large plate or pizza peel. Flip the whole thing over so that your loaf comes out of the proofing basket and is sitting on the plate. Artfully slash that loaf with the razor. Open up your oven, slide the loaf and parchment onto the middle of your baking stone, then carefully invert a pot or bowl over the loaf. (If using a Dutch oven, leave out the parchment, and just be careful not to burn yourself.) Bake for 20 minutes, then take the hot pot or bowl off your loaf (or remove the Dutch oven lid), and remove the parchment. Bake for another 15 minutes, and check the bread to see how it's looking. If it's not dark brown, give it another 5 to 10 minutes.

13. Take it out, and place it on a cooling rack or lean it against something so the air can move around it. When it's cool, enjoy.

WHAT YOU'LL NEED

FOODSTUFF	TOOLS
sourdough starter	measuring spoons
water	measuring cups
whole-wheat flour	thermometer (optional)
bread flour	big mixing bowl
sea salt, fine grind	mixing spoon
rice flour	plate or plastic wrap (to cover bowl)
cornmeal (optional)	spatula or bench knife
	proofing basket and cloth
	baking stone and oven-safe pot or bowl (at least 6 in/15 cm tall and 12 in/31 cm wide) OR a Dutch oven
	parchment paper (optional)
	large plate or pizza peel
	double-edged razor blade and handle
	cooling rack (optional)

HEARTH SOURDOUGH №3

All right, for this loaf we're going to follow a very similar approach to the last recipe, but this time we're going to focus on shaping and proofing. Shaping loaves is one of the trickier parts of baking—the only way you get good at it is by doing it over and over and over. But have no fear— I'm going to coach you through this, step by step.

For more in-depth instructions on preparing your dough up to the shaping, check out Lesson 7.

1. Gather your foodstuff and tools.

2. Make the pre-ferment. Measure and mix:

	1 LOAF	2 LOAVES	4 LOAVES
sourdough starter	1 Tbsp/ 15 g	2 Tbsp/ 30 g	¼ cup/ 60 g
cool water (60°F/15°C)	½ cup/ 120 g	1 cup/ 240 g	2 cups/ 480 g
whole-wheat flour	¾ cup/ 105 g	1½ cups/ 210 g	3 cups/ 420 g

3. Let it ferment. Cover the bowl with a plate or plastic wrap, and put it in a cool place (55 to 60°F/13 to 15°C) for about 12 hours.

4. Mix the dough. Mix in:

	1 LOAF	2 LOAVES	4 LOAVES
lukewarm water (80°F/27°C)	1 cup/ 240 g	2 cups/ 480 g	4 cups/ 960 g
bread flour	2½ cups/ 375 g	5 cups/ 750 g	10 cups/ 1,500 g
sea salt, fine grind	2 tsp/ 12 g	4 tsp/ 24 g	2 Tbsp plus 2 tsp/ 48 g

Roll up your sleeve, and mush it up real nice.

5. Knead the dough. After ½ hour, give your dough its first kneading—dip your hand in a bowl of water, then reach down into the side of the dough bowl, grab a little bit of it, and pull it up and push it down on top of the dough. Rotate the bowl a little bit and do it again. Give the dough about ten stretches and folds. Cover the dough, and let it sit for ½ hour.

6. Knead a few more times. After ½ hour, stretch and fold the dough another ten times. Cover the dough, and leave it alone for another ½ hour or so. Do this another two times, at 15- to 30-minutes intervals.

7. Let the magic happen. Cover the bowl and let the magic happen until it has increased in size by half. (Remember the last recipe? Here's where you get to apply what you learned.)

Here's where the two roads diverge in the yellow wood— we're gonna take the one less traveled.

8. Pre-shape your loaf. Flour your counter and pour the dough out. Gently fold a corner up and over into the middle, and repeat around the entire piece of dough. Flip your loaf so that it's seam-side down. Let it rest for 10 minutes.

↘ A very good question!

WHY ARE WE SHAPING THE DOUGH TWICE IN THIS RECIPE?

Up until now we've been taking a little shortcut at this point in the bread-baking process. But no more short-cuts. We're on a quest for the perfect loaf, and that quest does not have shortcuts. But I'm being dramatic—really, we are just going to shape the loaf twice. The first time you do it, it is called the "pre-shape," and the second time is called the "final shape." By shaping it twice, you are able to develop more tension in the loaf, and it can rise taller and prouder, and in turn so will you.

9. Shape your loaf. Now for the final shaping. Sprinkle a small handful of flour on top of the dough, and use your spatula or bench knife to flip it on its head, so that the seam is facing up. With palms facing upward, use both hands to grab the dough on the side nearest you.

Gently lift the dough off the table, letting gravity stretch it downward.

Put the dough back on the table, and fold the dough in your hands forward about two-thirds of the way up the loaf, leaving a lip of wet dough (about 1 in/ 2.5 cm wide) at the top.

Gently grab the top of the dough, and stretch it upward, then fold it downward about two-thirds of the way across the loaf. Now the loaf should be 8 to 12 in/ 20 to 31 cm across, with a seam from left to right.

Rotate the loaf a quarter turn, so the seam is going top to bottom.

Grab the side of the dough farthest from you and very gently roll it toward you, carefully rolling the dough into a ball, with the seam on the bottom.

10. Prepare the proofing basket and plop in your loaf. Rub rice flour into your proofing cloth, line your proofing basket with the cloth, and use your spatula or bench knife to plop your loaf into the basket, seam-side up.

11. Let your loaf rise. If you want to bake bread in about 3 hours, let the loaf sit out somewhere in your kitchen. Or if you want to bake bread anywhere from 6 to 24 hours later, stick the loaf in the fridge (or just outside if it's cool out—about 45°F/7°C).

12. Check the loaf's volume. The best way to decide if your loaf is ready to bake is by seeing how much it has increased in size, and by poking it with your finger. This can be a tricky decision to make when you first start baking, but for your first few loaves you should err on the side of baking it too early rather than too late (see the explanation given later for the reason). A good rule of thumb is that the loaf should be about 150 percent of its original size when you put it in the oven. How long

this will take depends on a bunch of different things—it can be as little as an hour (in a warm kitchen) and up to 2 days (in a cool fridge), depending on how the dough was prepared and what the temperature is where it's proofing. The same rule applies here as always: Hotter = faster, and cooler = slower.

→ A very good question!

WHAT HAPPENS IF I LET MY LOAF PROOF FOR TOO LONG?

This can really ruin your day. If you've done everything else right, your loaf consists of a nice lump of stretchy dough, with plenty of life in it that will rise in the hours before being baked, and then one last big rise in the oven, leading to a loaf that stands tall and proud and delicious. But if you let your loaf proof for too long, everything comes crashing down. It's helpful to think of the gluten in the dough as a system of balloons. You want the gluten to be stretched enough so that there are some nice-size air holes in your bread, and in order for this to happen the gluten has to be good and stretchy. But just like a balloon, the gluten will pop if it is stretched too far. And once it is popped, there's no way to reinflate it. So what happens is that your loaf comes out flat, with a rubbery, pale crust. This type of thing happens to every baker once in a while. Don't get too sad—it's a learning experience. Just don't ever, ever, EVER let it happen again.

WHAT HAPPENS IF I DON'T LET MY LOAF PROOF FOR LONG ENOUGH?

In general, this is much less catastrophic. Usually you just end up with a loaf of bread that is more dense than you'd like. This is because you haven't given the yeast enough time to do its thing, producing carbon dioxide that blows up the little gluten balloons. Once the dough goes into the oven, the loaf undergoes one last period of expansion, primarily due to the expanding gases in the existing holes. You'd much rather have an underproofed loaf than an overproofed loaf—one is just a little dense, but the other is a flat, rubbery, pancake loaf.

The rest of this recipe is the same as the previous one—you know how to do it.

13. Preheat. Once your loaf has risen, put your baking stone or Dutch oven on the middle rack of your oven and preheat at 475°F/240°C for 45 minutes.

14. Bake your bread. Sprinkle the loaf with cornmeal or cover with parchment paper, and invert your loaf onto the large plate or pizza peel. (Or carefully plop your loaf into the preheated Dutch oven.) Slash the top with the razor, get it into the oven, and cover it with a pot or bowl (or the Dutch oven lid). Bake for 20 minutes, uncover, and remove the parchment. Bake for another 15 minutes, and check the bread to see how it's looking. If it's not dark brown, give it another 5 to 10 minutes.

15. Once it's done, let it cool by placing it on a cooling rack or lean it against something so the air can move around it. Then surprise your neighbor with your new, hot loaf.

WHAT YOU'LL NEED

FOODSTUFF	TOOLS
sourdough starter	measuring spoons
water	measuring cups
whole-wheat flour	thermometer (optional)
bread flour	big mixing bowl (at least 6 in/15 cm tall and 12 in/31 cm wide)
sea salt, fine grind	mixing spoon
rice flour	plate or plastic wrap (to cover bowl)
cornmeal (optional)	spatula or bench knife
	proofing basket and cloth
	baking stone and oven-safe pot or bowl (at least 6 in/15 cm tall and 12 in/31 cm wide) OR a Dutch oven
	parchment paper (optional)
	large plate or pizza peel
	double-edged razor blade and handle
	cooling rack (optional)

HEARTH SOURDOUGH №4

I firmly believe in the benefits of a "bold bake." By baking your bread until most of its crust is a deep, dark brown, you coax out all of the possible flavors from the dough, create a glorious contrast between crunchy outside and soft inside, and also protect the loaf against quickly drying out. This can be a little unnerving at first, as it requires pushing the loaf right up to the cusp of being burnt, but it's worth the reward. I've included some nice photos here, so that you've got something to shoot for.

For more in-depth instructions on preparing your dough up to the baking, check out Lesson 8.

1. Gather your foodstuff and tools.

2. Make the pre-ferment. Measure and mix:

	1 LOAF	2 LOAVES	4 LOAVES
sourdough starter	1 Tbsp/ 15 g	2 Tbsp/ 30 g	¼ cup/ 60 g
cool water (60°F/15°C)	½ cup/ 120 g	1 cup/ 240 g	2 cups/ 480 g
whole-wheat flour	¾ cup/ 105 g	1½ cups/ 210 g	3 cups/ 420 g

3. Let it ferment. Cover the bowl with a plate or plastic wrap, and put it in a cool place (55 to 60°F/13 to 15°C) for about 12 hours.

4. Mix the dough. Mix in:

	1 LOAF	2 LOAVES	4 LOAVES
lukewarm water (80°F/27°C)	1 cup/ 240 g	2 cups/ 480 g	4 cups/ 960 g
bread flour	2½ cups/ 375 g	5 cups/ 750 g	10 cups/ 1,500 g
sea salt, fine grind	2 tsp/ 12 g	4 tsp/ 24 g	2 Tbsp plus 2 tsp/ 48 g

Roll up your sleeve, and mush it up real nice.

5. Knead the dough. After ½ hour, give your dough its first kneading—dip your hand in a bowl of water, then reach down into the side of the dough bowl, grab a little bit of it, and pull it up and push it down on top of the dough. Rotate the bowl a little bit and do it again. Give the dough about ten stretches and folds. Cover the dough, and let it sit for ½ hour.

6. Knead a few more times. After ½ hour, stretch and fold the dough another ten times. Cover the dough, and leave it alone for another ½ hour or so. Do this another two times, at 15- to 30-minute intervals.

7. Let the magic happen. Cover the bowl and let the magic happen until your dough is increased in volume by half.

8. Pre-shape your loaf. Flour your counter and pour the dough out. Gently fold a corner up and over into the middle, and repeat around the entire piece of dough. Flip your loaf so that it's seam-side down. Let it rest for 10 minutes.

9. Shape your loaf. You know how to do this, just as you did last time. (If you need a photographic refresher, refer to page 71.) Sprinkle a small handful of flour on top of the dough, and use your spatula or bench knife to flip it on its head, so that the seam is facing up. With palms facing upward, use both hands to grab the dough on the side nearest you. Gently lift the dough off the table, letting gravity stretch it downward. Put the dough back on the table, and fold the dough in your hands forward about two-thirds of the way up the loaf, leaving a lip of wet dough (about 1 in/2.5 cm wide) at the top. Grab both the left and right sides of the dough at the same time and stretch them outward until the dough is 8 to 12 in/20 to 31 cm across. Quickly fold in one side about two-thirds of the way, followed by the other side. Grab the side of the dough nearest you and roll the dough up into a log, taking care to create a seal on the small lip of dough that you created with your very first fold. Gently rock the loaf forward and back and get pumped.

10. Prepare the proofing basket and plop in your loaf. Rub rice flour into your proofing cloth and line the proofing basket with it. Use your spatula or bench knife to plop your loaf into the basket, seam-side up.

11. Let your loaf rise. Remember what you learned from the previous recipe—you get to decide when the loaf is ready for baking, based on its volume. About 150 percent of its original size is good.

12. Preheat. Once your loaf has risen, put your baking stone or Dutch oven on the middle rack of your oven and preheat at 475°F/240°C for 45 minutes.

13. Bake your bread. Sprinkle the loaf with cornmeal or cover with parchment paper, and invert your loaf onto the large plate or pizza peel. (Or carefully plop your loaf into the preheated Dutch oven.) Slash the top with the razor, get it into the oven, and cover it with a pot or bowl (or Dutch oven lid). Bake for 20 minutes, uncover, and remove the parchment. Bake for another 15 minutes, and check the bread to see how it's looking.

A little underbaked

14. Decide when your loaf is properly baked. People have different opinions on what constitutes a fully baked loaf of bread. One of the most common tests is the "thump test." This is done by picking up the loaf, thumping on the bottom, and listening for a "hollow" sound. This is a great way to check, but it's not enough. You want to make sure the bread is baked all the way through, but you also want to make sure that the crust has gotten dark enough to get the full flavor potential from the loaf.

way underbaked. This loaf was taken out of the oven about 15 minutes too early. The crust is still pale, and the insides of the loaf are not fully baked. This will not be a pleasant loaf to eat.

just right

a little underbaked. This loaf is perfectly edible, but you're going to miss out on the full benefits of a bold bake, particularly the super-crunchy and full-flavored crust.

just right. Perfection! The crust is nice and dark in most spots, but with other areas of light brown and gold. The inside is fully baked but still light and moist.

a little overbaked. We went just a touch too far on this one. The crust is going to taste a bit burnt, and too much water has evaporated out of the loaf, leading to a tough interior.

A little overbaked

way overbaked. Obviously, this is inedible. But the pigs'll eat it, or it'll make a nice addition to your garden.

15. Take it out and let it cool.

Good things come to loaves who wait. :)

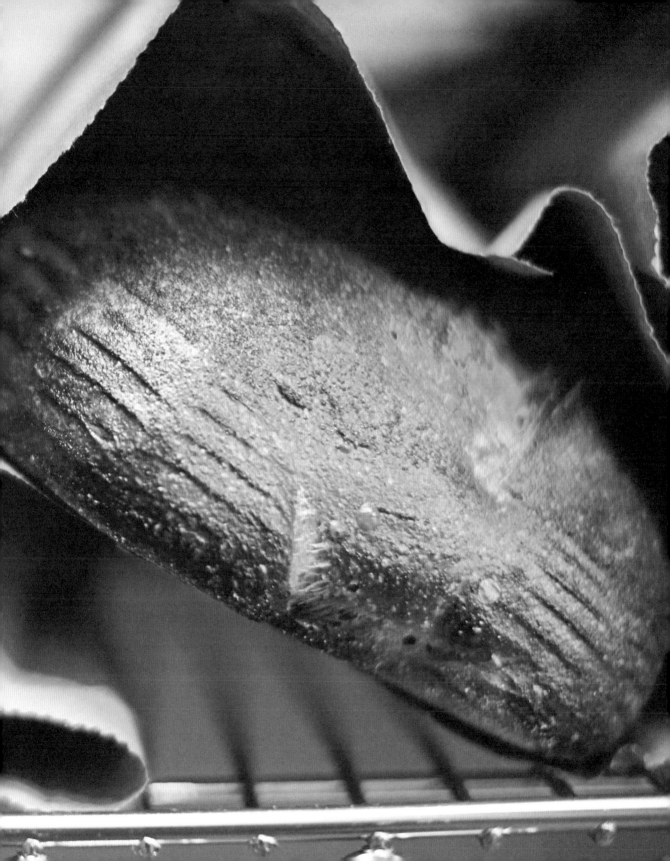

CHAPTER 3

A NEW CHALLENGE / ADDING STUFF TO BREAD

Baking bread wasn't really a choice, nor a chore—it was just what I wanted to be doing all the time. Any free time I had, I was baking bread, or reading about bread, or talking about bread, or daydreaming about bread. It was like when you first get a new girlfriend or boyfriend—you stay up late with them, even though you know you're going to be so, so tired tomorrow and you really shouldn't, but you just can't help yourself. And then somehow you actually aren't tired the next day, because you're just so excited about your new buddy, and you can't wait for the day to pass so that you can get back to hanging out with them into the early morning. This is what it was like with me and bread. We were just in love with each other so hard.

After selling loaves to friends and coworkers for a couple of months, I decided to try something that I hadn't heard of before: a bread subscription. I came up with this idea because I was having trouble predicting how much bread to bake for people. Most of the time I didn't bake enough, and then people would be disappointed that there wasn't any bread for them to buy. But once in a while I baked too much, and then I had leftover loaves, which was a total bummer. So why not see if people would prepay for a handful of loaves, so I'd know exactly how much to bake? This wasn't a novel idea—farmers have been doing subscription-based produce sales for years, but I'd never heard of anybody doing it with bread.

So one day I sent out an e-mail to my coworkers, excitedly announcing my Community Supported Bread (CSB) program. And they loved it! Within a few hours I had fifteen people sign up, and the bread subscription was born. After a few weeks of this, I expanded the bread subscription to a small shop a few blocks from my house, Gravel & Gold. It was touch and go for the first month or so, and then I got an e-mail outta the blue from an online food newsletter, Daily Candy. They wanted to write a story about me.

Are you kidding? Write a story? About me and my bread?!?!?!

WHOAWHOAWHOA!!!!

Ahem, I mean, why, yes, I could see agreeing to such a thing.

Anyway, the article came out, and all of the sudden twenty-five strangers had signed up to receive a loaf every week. I couldn't believe it. Strangers were buying my bread! This is for real! This is amazing!!!! Now I just had to figure out how to make all the different types of bread I'd promised.

One afternoon in the summer of 2010, I had just finished lunch at one of my favorite restaurants in the city, Outerlands. They make an absolutely killer sourdough sandwich loaf, and I'm sure I had eaten four or five slices. Dave, the owner of Outerlands, is a supersweet dude, and a friendship grew between us, with bread at its center. Dave was really generous with his bread knowledge, even letting me come in and attempt to shape loaves with him, which I did, badly. Anyway, I adored Dave's bread and had been working on replicating it at home for a month or so. I'd gotten close, but I was also beginning to wonder about making other kinds of bread—bread that had yummy things in it, like seeds.

I meandered into the co-op across the street from Outerlands, and took a gander at their bulk bins. I randomly grabbed a few types of seeds, in a ratio that matched their prices—sunflower seeds, flax seeds, and pumpkin seeds. I went home and tossed them into my dough, and I was floored—it worked! The bread was delicious! Aside from being excited, I was flabbergasted—is this how bakers make different types of bread? By just throwing in random stuff? I would come to learn that it was a bit more nuanced than this, and I had experienced a bit of beginner's luck, but the theory stuck with me: Toss random stuff in and you will absolutely stumble upon some stellar new breads.

Since that first seed combo, which came to be known as Seed Feast (as per the suggestion of my main "biznazz" associate and jazz drummer extraordinaire, Alex Snydman), I've tried out many different bread additives. Some worked better than others, so I'm going to spare you the trial and error. Following are a handful of my favorites.

And let me be clear—this *is* as easy as it looks. All you do is make the sourdough bread and fold in these ingredients. That's it. As always, if you're asking for my advice, I would suggest that you figure out how to make a sourdough hearth loaf that you're proud of before you start adding all sorts of wacky stuff to it. But you don't have to take my word for it.

oats

sesame seeds

bread flour

sunflower seeds

salt

cornmeal

flax seeds

yeast

WHAT YOU'LL NEED

FOODSTUFF	TOOLS
sunflower seeds	measuring cups
flax seeds	measuring spoons
pumpkin seeds	bowl or large jar
water	thermometer (optional)
sourdough starter	2 plates or plastic wrap (for covering bowls)
whole-wheat flour	big mixing bowl
bread flour	mixing spoon
sea salt, fine grind	proofing basket and cloth
rice flour	spatula or bench knife
cornmeal (optional)	baking stone and oven-safe pot or bowl (at least 6 in/15 cm tall and 12 in/31 cm wide) OR a Dutch oven
	parchment paper (optional)
	large plate or pizza peel
	double-edged razor blade and handle
	cooling rack (optional)

SEED FEAST

This was the very first bread I made with any-thing other than flour, water, and salt. I grabbed some seeds from the store and tossed them in my dough, doing everything else the same, and voilà—Seed Feast was born. This is still one of my favorite breads that I make, and I've heard the same from a lot of happy customers. I've never seen this seed combo in any other bread, and for this I feel very proud. It's a Josey Baker Bread original.

Aside from the addition of a seed soaker in this recipe, everything else is the same as the hearth sourdough on page 73.

1. Gather your foodstuff and tools.

2. Toast the seeds. Preheat your oven to 350°F/180°C. Spread all the seeds on a baking sheet and toast until they start to brown, about 15 minutes, stirring halfway through baking.

3. Make your seed soaker. Because seeds soak up a lot of water, you've gotta let them soak for a while before adding them to your dough. Put the following into a bowl or large jar:

	1 LOAF	2 LOAVES	4 LOAVES
sunflower seeds	½ cup/ 80 g	1 cup/ 160 g	2 cups/ 320 g
flax seeds	⅓ cup/ 55 g	⅔ cup/ 110 g	1⅓ cups/ 220 g
pumpkin seeds	¼ cup/ 40 g	½ cup/ 80 g	1 cup/ 160 g
hot water (100°F/38°C)	¾ cup/ 180 g	1½ cups/ 360 g	3 cups/ 720 g

Mix everything together and cover the bowl, so the water can't evaporate. (Drain before adding to your final dough.)

4. Make your sourdough pre-ferment. Use starter that is sour smelling in a good way, most likely between 12 and 24 hours old. Make your pre-ferment 8 to 12 hours before you want to start mixing your dough—likely in the evening before you go to bed or in the morning. You want it to be the consistency of thick pancake batter. Put this stuff in a big bowl:

	1 LOAF	2 LOAVES	4 LOAVES
sourdough starter	1 Tbsp/ 15 g	2 Tbsp/ 30 g	¼ cup/ 60 g
cool water (60°F/15°C)	½ cup/ 120 g	1 cup/ 240 g	2 cups/ 480 g
whole-wheat flour	¾ cup/ 105 g	1½ cups/ 210 g	3 cups/ 420 g

Mix it up real good. Cover with a plate or plastic wrap and leave it alone for 8 to 12 hours.

5. Mix the dough. Uncover the pre-ferment bowl, and take a big whiff. It should be putting off a pretty strong smell, nice and yummy, maybe a touch sour. If it doesn't, no biggie; it'll still make awesome bread. Add:

	1 LOAF	2 LOAVES	4 LOAVES
lukewarm water (80°F/27°C)	1 cup/ 240 g	2 cups/ 480 g	4 cups/ 960 g
bread flour	2½ cups/ 375 g	5 cups/ 750 g	10 cups/ 1,500 g
sea salt, fine grind	2 tsp/ 12 g	4 tsp/ 24 g	2 Tbsp plus 2 tsp/ 48 g
seed soaker, drained	all of it	all of it	all of it

Mix everything together so that it's evenly combined, just for 30 seconds to a minute. Cover with a plate or plastic wrap, and let it sit for 30 minutes to an hour, whatever is convenient.

6. Knead the dough. Dip your hand in a bowl of water, then reach down into the side of the dough bowl, grab a little bit of it, and pull it up and push it down on top of the dough. Rotate the bowl a little bit and do it again to another portion of the dough. Give the dough about ten stretches and folds. Cover the dough, and let it sit for ½ hour.

7. Stretch and fold a few more times. After ½ hour, stretch and fold the dough another ten times. Cover the dough, and leave it alone for another ½ hour or so. Do this another two times, at 15- to 30-minute intervals.

8. Choose your own path. Choose your own adventure for the **bulk rise.**

If you want to shape your loaf in 2 to 3 hours, let the dough sit out somewhere in your kitchen.

If you want to shape your loaf anywhere from 12 to 48 hours later, stick it in the fridge (or just outside if it's cool out—about 45°F/7°C).

9. Shape your loaf. After the dough has completed its bulk rise, flour your counter and dump out the dough. Pre-shape your loaf into a round, then let it rest for 10 to 15 minutes. Shape it into a loaf and leave it on your counter, seam-side down, while you line the proofing basket with a rice-floured cloth. Plop it into the prepared basket, seam-side up.

10. Choose your own path. Choose your own adventure for the **final rise**.

If you want to bake bread in 2 to 3 hours, let the loaf sit out somewhere in your kitchen.

If you want to bake bread anywhere from 6 to 24 hours later, stick the loaf in the fridge (or just outside if it's cool out—about 45°F/7°C).

11. Preheat. Once your loaf has risen, put your baking stone or Dutch oven on the middle rack of your oven and preheat at 475°F/240°C for 45 minutes.

12. Bake your bread. Sprinkle the loaf with cornmeal (or cover with parchment paper), and invert your loaf onto the large plate or pizza peel. (Or carefully plop your loaf into your preheated Dutch oven.) Slash the top with the razor, get it into the oven, and cover it with a pot or bowl (or the Dutch oven lid). Bake for 20 minutes, uncover, and bake for another 25 minutes. Check the bread and see how it's looking. If it's not dark brown, give it another 5 to 10 minutes.

13. Let it cool by placing it on a cooling rack or leaning it against something so the air can move around it. When it's cool, enjoy.

Want a surefire
way to make
delicious bread?
FILL IT WITH CHEESE.

WHAT YOU'LL NEED

FOODSTUFF	TOOLS
sourdough starter	measuring spoons
water	measuring cup
whole-wheat flour	thermometer (optional)
Parmesan or Grana Padano cheese	big mixing bowl
freshly ground black pepper	mixing spoon
bread flour	plate or plastic wrap (for covering bowl)
sea salt, fine grind	sharp knife
rice flour	grater
cornmeal (optional)	electric spice grinder or pepper mill
	proofing basket and cloth
	spatula or bench knife
	baking stone and oven-safe pot or bowl (at least 6 in/15 cm tall and 12 in/31 cm wide) OR a Dutch oven
	parchment paper (optional)
	large plate or pizza peel
	double-edged razor blade and handle
	cooling rack (optional)

BLACK PEPPER PARMESAN

This bread was a childhood favorite of mine, baked by a great small bakery in Vermont. I can remember my mom and me eating slice after slice of toast slathered with butter, the hunks of Parmesan melted and oozing all over. Then one day the bakery stopped making it, and we were so sad. I didn't have it again until the day I decided to have a go at making my own version. I mean, let's be honest—putting cheese IN bread

is a pretty good way to make it delicious. And the black pepper—it's just perfect. This isn't really an everyday bread, but for a special occasion it's phenomenal.

Aside from the addition of the cheese and black pepper in this recipe, everything else is the same as the hearth sourdough on page 73.

1. **Gather your foodstuff and tools.**

2. **Make your sourdough pre-ferment.** Use starter that is sour smelling in a good way, most likely between 12 and 24 hours old. Make your sourdough pre-ferment 8 to 12 hours before you want to start mixing your dough. (I usually do it either when I wake up or right before I go to bed.) You're aiming to make your sourdough pre-ferment to be the consistency of thick pancake batter. Put this stuff in a big bowl:

	1 LOAF	2 LOAVES	4 LOAVES
sourdough starter	1 Tbsp/ 15 g	2 Tbsp/ 30 g	¼ cup/ 60 g
cool water (60°F/15°C)	½ cup/ 120 g	1 cup/ 240 g	2 cups/ 480 g
whole-wheat flour	¾ cup/ 105 g	1½ cups/ 210 g	3 cups/ 420 g

Mix it up real good. Cover with a plate or plastic wrap and leave it alone for 8 to 12 hours.

3. **Cut the cheese, grind the pepper.** You can use Parmesan cheese or Grana Padano or really whatever cheese you like, but I prefer a sharp, aged cheese. Coarsely chop about half of it into roughly ½-in/12-mm cubes and grate the rest of it, or just chop it into very small pieces. Grind the pepper right before adding it to your dough, so you get all of the great peppery flavor. Use an electric spice grinder or a good old-fashioned pepper mill.

	1 LOAF	2 LOAVES	4 LOAVES
Parmesan or Grana Padano cheese, half cubed and half grated	½ cup/ 60 g	1 cup/ 120 g	2 cups/ 240 g
black pepper, freshly ground	2 tsp	4 tsp	2 Tbsp plus 2 tsp

Mix it in when you make your final dough.

4. **Mix the dough.** Uncover the bowl of pre-ferment, and take a big whiff. It should be putting off a pretty strong smell, nice and yummy, maybe a touch sour. If it doesn't, no biggie; it'll still make awesome bread. Add:

	1 LOAF	2 LOAVES	4 LOAVES
lukewarm water (80°F/27°C)	1 cup/ 240 g	2 cups/ 480 g	4 cups/ 960 g
bread flour	2½ cups/ 375 g	5 cups/ 750 g	10 cups/ 1,500 g
sea salt, fine grind	2 tsp/ 12 g	4 tsp/ 24 g	2 Tbsp plus 2 tsp/ 48 g
cheese and pepper	all of it	all of it	all of it

Mix everything together so that it's evenly combined, just for 30 seconds to a minute. Cover with a plate or plastic wrap, and let it sit for 30 minutes to an hour, whatever is convenient.

5. **Knead the dough.** Dip your hand in a bowl of water, then reach down into the side of the dough bowl, grab a little bit of it, and pull it up and push it down on top of the dough. Rotate the bowl a little bit and do it again to another portion of the dough. Give the dough about ten stretches and folds. Cover the dough, and let it sit for ½ hour.

6. **Stretch and fold a few more times.** After ½ hour, stretch and fold the dough another ten times. Cover the dough, and leave it alone for another ½ hour or so. Do this another two times, at 15- to 30-minute intervals.

7. Choose your own path. Choose your own adventure for the **bulk rise**.

If you want to shape your loaf in 2 to 3 hours, let the dough sit out somewhere in your kitchen.

If you want to shape your loaf anywhere from 12 to 48 hours later, stick it in the fridge (or just outside if it's cool out—about 45°F/7°C).

8. Shape your loaf. After the dough has completed its bulk rise, flour your counter and dump out the dough. Pre-shape your loaf into a round, then let it rest for 10 to 15 minutes. Shape it into a loaf and leave it on your counter, seam-side down, while you line the proofing basket with a rice-floured cloth. Plop it into your prepared basket, seam-side up.

9. Choose your own path. Choose your own adventure for the **final rise**.

If you want to bake bread in 2 to 3 hours, let the loaf sit out somewhere in your kitchen.

If you want to bake bread anywhere from 6 to 24 hours later, stick the loaf in the fridge (or just outside if it's cool out—about 45°F/7°C).

10. Preheat. Once your loaf has risen, put your baking stone or Dutch oven on the middle rack of your oven and preheat at 475°F/240°C for 45 minutes.

11. Bake your bread. Sprinkle the loaf with cornmeal or cover with parchment paper, and invert your loaf onto the large plate or pizza peel. (Or carefully plop the loaf into the Dutch oven.) Slash the top with the razor, get it into the oven, and cover it with a pot or bowl (or Dutch oven lid). Bake for 20 minutes, uncover, and remove the parchment. Bake for another 25 minutes. Check the bread and see how it's looking. If it's not dark brown, give it another 7 minutes.

12. Let it cool by placing it on a cooling rack or leaning it against something so the air can move around it. When it's cool, enjoy.

your grandma
is gonna love
this one!

WHAT YOU'LL NEED

FOODSTUFF	TOOLS
sourdough starter	measuring spoons
water	measuring cups
whole-wheat flour	thermometer (optional)
sesame seeds	big mixing bowl
brown poppy seeds	mixing spoon
bread flour	2 plates or plastic wrap (for covering bowls)
sea salt, fine grind	small bowl or jar
cornmeal (optional)	spatula or bench knife
	small towel
	proofing basket and cloth
	baking stone and oven-safe pot or bowl (at least 6 in/15 cm tall and 12 in/31 cm wide) OR a Dutch oven
	parchment paper (optional)
	large plate or pizza peel
	double-edged razor blade and handle
	cooling rack (optional)

SESAME POPPY

This bread reminds me of an everything bagel, which in my humble opinion is the best type of bagel. I don't think that I had ever actually had a sesame poppy loaf like this before I made one, but it's an undeniable classic, a go-to bread that will stand the test of time. Bake it up, then use it for toast or as a sandwich bread, or let that sucker get stale and turn it into French toast. Just be sure to tell 'em that Josey Baker sent ya.

Aside from the addition of the seeds in this recipe, everything else is the same as the hearth sourdough on page 73.

1. Gather your foodstuff and tools.

2. Toast the seeds. Preheat the oven to 350°F/180°C. Spread all the seeds on a baking sheet and toast for about 15 minutes, until they are just starting to brown.

3. Make your sourdough pre-ferment. Use starter that is sour smelling in a good way, most likely between 12 and 24 hours old. Make your pre-ferment 8 to 12 hours before you want to start mixing your dough—likely in the evening before you go to bed or in the morning. You want it to be the consistency of thick pancake batter. Put this stuff in a big bowl:

	1 LOAF	2 LOAVES	4 LOAVES
sourdough starter	1 Tbsp/ 15 g	2 Tbsp/ 30 g	1/4 cup/ 60 g
cool water (60°F/15°C)	1/2 cup/ 120 g	1 cup/ 240 g	2 cups/ 480 g
whole-wheat flour	3/4 cup/ 105 g	1 1/2 cups/ 210 g	3 cups/ 420 g

Mix it up real good. Cover with a plate or plastic wrap and leave it alone for 8 to 12 hours.

4. Make your seed soaker. Because seeds soak up a lot of water, you've gotta let them soak for a while before adding them to your dough. Put the following into a small bowl or jar:

	1 LOAF	2 LOAVES	4 LOAVES
toasted sesame seeds	1/2 cup/ 80 g	1 cup/ 160 g	2 cups/ 320 g
poppy seeds	1/3 cup/ 55 g	2/3 cup/ 110 g	1 1/3 cups/ 220 g
hot water (100°F/38°C)	1/2 cup/ 120 g	1 cup/ 240 g	2 cups/ 480 g

Cover this stuff and set it aside. (Drain before adding to your final dough.)

5. Mix the dough. Uncover the pre-ferment bowl, and take a big whiff. It should be putting off a pretty strong smell, nice and yummy, maybe a touch sour. If it doesn't, no biggie; it'll still make awesome bread. Add:

	1 LOAF	2 LOAVES	4 LOAVES
lukewarm water (80°F/27°C)	1 cup/ 240 g	2 cups/ 480 g	4 cups/ 960 g
bread flour	2 1/2 cups/ 375 g	5 cups/ 750 g	12 cups/ 1,500 g
sea salt, fine grind	2 tsp/ 12 g	4 tsp/ 24 g	2 Tbsp plus 2 tsp/ 48 g
seed soaker, drained	all of it	all of it	all of it

Mix everything together so that it's evenly combined, just for 30 seconds to a minute. Cover with a plate or plastic wrap, and let it sit for 30 minutes to an hour, whatever is convenient.

6. Knead the dough. Dip your hand in a bowl of water, then reach down into the side of the dough bowl, grab a little bit of it, and pull it up and push it down on top of the dough. Rotate the bowl a little bit and do it again to another portion of the dough. Give the dough about ten stretches and folds. Cover the dough, and let it sit for 1/2 hour.

7. Knead a few more times. After 1/2 hour, stretch and fold the dough another ten times. Cover the dough, and leave it alone for another 1/2 hour or so. Do this another two times, at 15- to 30-minute intervals.

8. Choose your own path. Choose your own adventure for the **bulk rise**.

If you want to shape your loaf in 3 to 4 hours, let the dough sit out somewhere in your kitchen.

If you want to shape your loaf anywhere from 12 to 48 hours later, stick it in the fridge (or just outside if it's cool out—about 45°F/7°C).

9. Pre-shape your loaf. Flour your counter and pour the dough out. Gently fold a corner up and over into the middle, and repeat around the entire piece of dough. Flip your loaf so that it's seam-side down. Let it rest for 10 minutes.

10. Shape your loaf. You know how to do this, just as you did last time. If you need a refresher, refer to page 71.

11. Cover your loaf in seeds. Let your loaf rest, seam-side down, while you prepare to cover it with seeds.

Wet a small towel, gently wring it out, and spread it out on a plate.

Take ½ cup/80 g of sesame seeds and ¼ cup/35 g of poppy seeds, and spread them out on another plate.

Gently lift up your loaf, and roll it in the wet towel to dampen it.

Now carefully roll your wet loaf in the bed of seeds, getting it completely covered.

Plop it into your UNFLOURED cloth-lined proofing basket, seam-side up.

12. Choose your own path. Choose your own adventure for the **final rise**.

If you want to bake bread in 2 to 3 hours, let the loaf sit out somewhere in your kitchen.

If you want to bake bread anywhere from 6 to 24 hours later, stick the loaf in the fridge (or just outside if it's cool out—about 45°F/7°C).

13. Preheat. Once your loaf has risen, put your baking stone or Dutch oven on the middle rack of your oven and preheat at 475°F/240°C for 45 minutes.

14. Bake your bread. Sprinkle the loaf with cornmeal (or cover with parchment paper), and invert it onto the large plate or pizza peel. (Or carefully plop the loaf into your preheated Dutch oven.) Slash the top with the razor, get it into the oven, and cover it with a pot or bowl (or the Dutch oven lid). Bake for 20 minutes, uncover, and bake for another 25 minutes. Check the bread to see how it's looking. If it's not dark brown, give it another 5 to 10 minutes.

15. Let it cool by placing it on a cooling rack or leaning it against something so the air can move around it. When it's cool, enjoy.

toasting seeds before adding
them to the bread is a pain,
but, man oh man, it's
well worth it. TRUST ME.

CHAPTER 4

EAT BREAD EVERY DAY / WHOLE-WHEAT BREADS

My best buddy and longtime housemate Rafi has been experimenting with whole grains and fermentation and general back-to-the-land stuff for years. His vibes foster strong resonant frequencies, you could say, as long as you say it with a smirk. He's a gifted man with a razor-sharp intellect, an unfair amount of creativity, and the ability to do the most pull-ups I have ever seen anyone do. He also has that rare ability to make suggestions that I often see as silly, but I later think about again and say, "Oh yeah, now I know what he's talking about. That's a really good idea."

(One funny and stupid example of me accompanying him on one of his not-so-genius experiments was when he suggested that we go for a four-day backpacking trip in the Lost Coast of Northern California, bringing only pemmican to eat. For those of you who don't know—which is most of you, I assume—pemmican is a Native American foodstuff made of rendered fat, slow-cooked lean meat, and maybe, if you're lucky, some dried fruits and nuts. Rafi made a handful of pemmican pucks and wrapped them in plastic wrap, and we tossed them in our backpacks and took off. On day one we were feeling strong and proud, but by day two we were tired of the disgusting, greasy pucks. That's when I surprised him with a candy bar that I'd smuggled in. On day four we refused to eat any more of the stuff and hiked furiously for four hours and broke the speed limit to get to a restaurant, where we ate several brunches apiece and quickly passed out on a bench outside.)

Ever since the beginning of my bread-baking love affair, Rafi had been insistent that I should be making and eating more whole-grain bread. And he wasn't talking about "whole-grain bread" that is really white bread with a little bit of whole grains tossed in for show. He was talking about real, live whole-grain bread—bread made solely from whole grains, like whole wheat, or rye, or whatever, really. I categorized whole-grain bread as

something that was very, very tricky, a bread reserved for master bakers and/or hippies, and I believed that even they had difficulty making one that wasn't a dense brick fit only for horses. Oh how wrong I was.

I found a recipe on the Internet, took a stab at it, and I'll be damned—it tasted incredible. And it wasn't dense as a brick! What did I do to make this magical whole-wheat bread? I will tell you in a minute, but first I want to tell you about the REAL first time I made whole-wheat bread, and how crappy it was.

I was in Rainbow Co-op, buying some flour for the fourth or fifth sourdough bread loaf I'd ever made. I was moseying around the bulk section, and I noticed the "whole-wheat bread flour." Not really knowing much about anything, I said to myself, "That looks nice. I will try to use that to make bread." So I did everything exactly the same way that I'd done it before, following that first recipe that George had scribbled for me. The dough definitely felt a bit stiffer than usual, but what the heck, I didn't care, nor did I know any better. When I brought the loaf to a party that night, it failed to garner the oohs and aahs that I'd come to find so gosh darned encouraging over the past several weeks. And I couldn't blame them—the bread was dense and dry and just really not very good.

What the heck did I do wrong?

What I didn't know then, but know now, is that whole-wheat flour demands a slightly different treatment than white flour. Basically, whole wheat is a thirsty flour—it soaks up a lot of water. This is because whole-wheat flour has the germ and bran in it, the parts of the wheat berry that are so awesome for you but also can go rancid quickly. They suck up water, and so when making a whole-wheat dough, you need more of it.

But here's another sweet thing about whole wheat—the microorganisms in sourdough just go bonkers for it. What I mean is the wild yeast and bacteria consume and reproduce much quicker, and so fermentation gallops along at a faster clip than with white bread. What does this mean? You just gotta be ready for it—either use cooler water or less starter, or be ready for things to happen faster. Luckily, you're a big kid, and I know you can handle it, just like I did.

some thoughts on picking a whole-wheat flour

There are a lot of things to consider when picking a whole-wheat flour for bread. Here are a few of the most important ones and some suggestions to ponder.

- **Get fresh—freshly milled.** Whole-wheat flour has all of the wheat berry in it, which demands a little more attention than white flour. Ya see, white flour (which is just made from the starchy part of the wheat berry, the "endosperm") has a really long shelf life. It's fine for many months, perhaps even a few years. But whole wheat is a different beast. It has the germ (oil and nutrient rich) and the bran (fiber rich) in there as well, and these things shorten the shelf life. In particular, the germ has oils that can go rancid within a month or two. The easiest way to ensure freshness is to buy whole-wheat flour from a store that sells a lot of it (check the date on the packaging) or to order it online and get it sent right to your home.

- **Get stoned—stone-ground.** (Believe it or not, this is a charged topic in certain circles, but here's my ridiculously abbreviated history of milling techniques, with a couple of my opinions scattered throughout.) In the old days, flour was made by grinding grains between stones. Then came big industry, and they figured out ways to make a lot more flour in a lot less time. Unfortunately, as is often the case with these types of things, there were some trade-offs. Stone milling keeps the grains and flour cool, which preserves all the nutrients, so that you can eat them and absorb them into your body. The new high-volume methods heat up the grains and flour and can speed up the degradation of the nutrients. People are working on ways to produce huge quantities of flour without degrading it at all, but if you want to be safe, just get stone-ground.

- **Get strong—pick "bread flour" or "high-protein flour," NOT "pastry flour" or "cake flour."** You want a flour that is meant for making bread, and typically these flours are labeled as "bread flour" or maybe just "whole-wheat flour." This is a little bit more important when dealing with whole-wheat flour because it contains both the bran and the germ of the wheat berry, neither of which contributes to the strength of the dough. Basically, you've got this other stuff in your bread that, while being very delicious and nutritious, doesn't contribute to making the dough any stretchier, or able to hold gas. So be sure to get bread flour, not something like pastry flour.

- **Get fine—fine grind.** Because the flour is ground into very small particles, you're able to make a bread that is amazingly light and airy for a whole-wheat bread. Why? The tricky thing about whole-wheat flour is that it has shards of bran in it, which act like little swords on the gluten matrix. The bigger the pieces of bran are, the more likely they are to pop the bubbles that form in your dough, and hence the more dense your bread is. When everything is ground to a fine powder, the bran isn't able to pop the bubbles as easily, and voilà! You get a whole-wheat bread that is, at its fullest potential, "lacy."

- **Get local—locally grown and locally milled (if possible).** Obviously, this totally depends on where you live, since wheat is not grown everywhere. But it's rad to support your neighbors, and it's probably easier to get it fresh if it was milled near you. This may mean making a compromise in terms of quality (or gluten content) of flour, but I will leave all that stuff up to you. Good wheat for bread is being grown in more and more places every year, such as upstate New York, Vermont, Oregon, California, and all over the middle and northwest of the country.

WHOLE-WHEAT BREADS SINCE 2010

BREAD MAKER

Roll the top of your
loaf in rolled oats
after you shape it.

WHAT YOU'LL NEED

FOODSTUFF	TOOLS
sourdough starter	measuring spoons
water	measuring cups
whole-wheat flour	thermometer (optional)
sea salt, fine grind	big mixing bowl
rice flour	mixing spoon
cornmeal (optional)	plate or plastic wrap (for covering bowl)
	proofing basket and cloth
	spatula or bench knife
	baking stone and oven-safe pot or bowl (at least 6 in/15 cm tall and 12 in/31 cm wide) OR a Dutch oven
	parchment paper (optional)
	large plate or pizza peel
	double-edged razor blade and handle
	cooling rack (optional)

100 PERCENT WHOLE WHEAT

Most "whole wheat" bread has plenty of white flour in it, not to mention a zillion other things, like corn syrup and coloring and preservatives and other crap I can't pronounce. You don't need that stuff. All you need is a little extra water and a little extra care, and you can make a super-delicious whole-wheat bread that is just that—the whole of the wheat berry and nothing more (of course, you should put salt in it too, unless you're some salt-hating weirdo). It's not going to be the lightest, airiest bread you've ever eaten, but some days you probably say to yourself, "Ya know what, light and airy bread is for wussies. I like my bread

a little darker, a little denser, a little stronger. Just like me." But stop talking to yourself, and start baking whole-wheat bread.

I wrote up this recipe as a hearth loaf, but you can just as easily go sandwich style. Ya see, YOU make up the rules now, baker.

1. Gather your foodstuff and tools.

2. **Make your sourdough pre-ferment.** Use starter that is sour smelling in a good way, most likely between 12 and 24 hours old. Make your pre-ferment 8 to

12 hours before you want to start mixing your dough—likely in the evening before you go to bed or in the morning. You want it to be the consistency of thick pancake batter. Put this stuff in a big bowl:

	1 LOAF	2 LOAVES	4 LOAVES
sourdough starter	1 tsp/ 6 g	2 tsp/ 12 g	4 tsp/ 24 g
cool water (60°F/15°C)	¼ cup/ 60 g	½ cup/ 120 g	1 cup/ 240 g
whole-wheat flour	⅓ cup/ 50 g	⅔ cup/ 100 g	1⅓ cups/ 200 g

Mix it up real good. Cover with a plate or plastic wrap and leave it alone for 8 to 12 hours.

➤ A very good question!

WHY AM I MAKING LESS SOURDOUGH PRE-FERMENT FOR THIS RECIPE THAN FOR THE OTHER BREADS?

Excellent question. You're so observant! Whole-wheat dough ferments faster than doughs made with white flour. Why? The microorganisms in your sourdough starter just go bonkers for that whole-wheat dough, just like your body does. To make this recipe fit what you've come to expect from the other recipes in this book, I suggest that you reduce the amount of sourdough pre-ferment when making this bread. But this isn't a hard and fast rule—if you wanna try to speed things up, you can use the same amount of sourdough pre-ferment that you've been using for the other sourdough bread recipes. But what's the rush? Take it nice and easy, and get pumped that you're tackling this hearty bread, once and for all.

---

3. Mix your dough. Uncover the bowl, and take a big whiff. It should be putting off a pretty strong smell, nice and yummy, maybe a touch sour. If it doesn't, no biggie; it'll still make awesome bread. Add:

	1 LOAF	2 LOAVES	4 LOAVES
lukewarm water (80°F/27°C)	1½ cups/ 360 g	3 cups/ 720 g	6 cups/ 1,440 g
whole-wheat flour	3¼ cups/ 455 g	6½ cups/ 910 g	13 cups/ 1,820 g
sea salt, fine grind	2 tsp/ 12 g	4 tsp/ 24 g	2 Tbsp plus 2 tsp/ 48 g

Stir it up with your strong hands 'til it's good and mixed together (30 seconds to a minute will do). Cover and let it sit for 30 minutes to an hour, whatever is convenient. Go for a walk or read a book or talk to a friend.

4. Knead the dough. After it sits for a while, the dough is ready to be kneaded. Dip your hand in a bowl of water, then reach down into the side of the dough bowl, grab a little bit of it, and pull it up and push it down on top of the dough. Rotate the bowl a little bit and do it again. Be sweet and gentle yet firm with the dough. Do this to all of the dough; it'll probably take about ten folds. Cover the dough, and let sit for ½ hour.

5. Stretch and fold a few more times. After ½ hour, stretch and fold the dough another ten times. Cover the dough, and leave it alone for another ½ hour or so. Do this another two times, at 15- to 30-minute intervals.

6. Choose your own path. Now you get to choose your own adventure for the **bulk rise**. Do what is convenient for you here.

If you want to shape your loaf in 2 to 3 hours, let the dough sit out somewhere in your kitchen.

If you want to shape your loaf anywhere from 12 to 48 hours later, stick it in the fridge (or just outside if it's cool out—about 45°F/7°C).

7. Shape your loaf. After the dough has completed its bulk rise, flour your counter and dump out the dough.

Pre-shape your loaf, then let it rest for 10 to 15 minutes. Shape it into a loaf and let it rest, seam-side down, while you line your proofing basket with a cloth that you've dusted with rice flour. Plop the loaf into the prepared proofing basket, seam-side up.

8. Choose your own path. Now you get to choose your own adventure for the **final rise**. Again, do what is convenient for you here, folks!

If you want to bake bread in 3 to 4 hours, let the loaf sit out somewhere in your kitchen.

If you want to bake bread anywhere from 6 to 24 hours later, stick the loaf in the fridge (or just outside if it's cool out—about 45°F/7°C).

9. Preheat. Put your baking stone or Dutch oven on the middle rack of your oven and preheat to 475°F/240°C for 45 minutes.

10. Bake your bread. Sprinkle the loaf with cornmeal (or cover with parchment paper), and invert your loaf onto the large plate or pizza peel. (Or carefully plop the loaf into your preheated Dutch oven.) Slash the top with the razor, get it into the oven, and cover it with a pot or bowl (or the Dutch oven lid). Bake for 20 minutes, uncover, and get excited that your dough is magically turning into delicious bread. Bake for another 25 minutes. Check the bread and see how it's looking. If it's not dark brown, give it another 7 minutes.

11. Let it cool. Whole-wheat bread really benefits from a little rest before you slice into it. Because it's such a wet dough, it can actually have a slightly gummy texture if it's not given proper time to mellow out after its bake. So just be patient, and give this loaf a couple of hours before tearing into it.

BAKER'S PERCENTAGE

Whole-wheat flour	100%
Water	83%
Salt	2.5%

WHAT YOU'LL NEED

FOODSTUFF	TOOLS
sourdough starter	measuring spoons
water	measuring cups
whole-wheat flour	thermometer (optional)
sesame seeds	big mixing bowl
poppy seeds	mixing spoon
sea salt, fine grind	small bowl or jar
cornmeal (optional)	2 plates or plastic wrap (for covering bowls)
	spatula or bench knife
	small towel
	proofing basket and cloth
	baking stone and oven-safe pot or bowl (at least 6 in/15 cm tall and 12 in/31 cm wide) OR a Dutch oven
	parchment paper (optional)
	large plate or pizza peel
	double-edged razor blade and handle
	cooling rack (optional)

WHOLE-WHEAT SESAME POPPY

Once you've got the straight-up, 100 percent whole-wheat loaf under your belt, you might wanna spice things up a bit by adding some seeds. This is a great combo that is surprisingly hard to find. I like to put just sesame seeds inside the loaf, then cover it with both sesame and poppy seeds, but you are your own baker, so do what you will.

I wrote up this recipe as a free-form hearth loaf, but you can just as easily go sandwich style.

1. Gather your foodstuff and tools.

2. Toast the seeds. Preheat your oven to 350°F/180°C. Spread the seeds on a baking sheet and toast until they start to brown, about 15 minutes, stirring halfway through baking.

Whole-wheat flour is darker than "white" flour because it has bran and germ in it.

3. Make your sourdough pre-ferment. Use starter that is sour smelling in a good way, most likely between 12 and 24 hours old. Make your pre-ferment 8 to 12 hours before you want to start mixing your dough—likely in the evening before you go to bed or in the morning. You want it to be the consistency of thick pancake batter. Put this stuff in a big bowl:

	1 LOAF	2 LOAVES	4 LOAVES
sourdough starter	1 tsp/ 6 g	2 tsp/ 12 g	4 tsp/ 24 g
cool water (60°F/15°C)	¼ cup/ 60 g	½ cup/ 120 g	1 cup/ 240 g
whole-wheat flour	⅓ cup/ 50 g	⅔ cup/ 100 g	1⅓ cups/ 200 g

Mix it up real good. Cover with a plate or plastic wrap and leave it alone for 8 to 12 hours.

4. Make a seed soaker. Pour the following into a small bowl or jar:

	1 LOAF	2 LOAVES	4 LOAVES
toasted sesame seeds	½ cup/ 80 g	1 cup/ 160 g	2 cups/ 320 g
hot water (100°F/38°C)	⅓ cup/ 80 g	⅔ cup/ 160 g	1⅓ cups/ 320 g

Cover this stuff and set it aside. (Drain before adding to your final dough.)

5. Mix your dough. Uncover the big bowl, and take a big whiff. It should be putting off a pretty strong smell, nice and yummy, maybe a touch sour. If it doesn't, no biggie; it'll still make awesome bread. Add:

	1 LOAF	2 LOAVES	4 LOAVES
lukewarm water (80°F/27°C)	1½ cups/ 360 g	3 cups/ 720 g	6 cups/ 1,440 g
whole-wheat flour	3¼ cups/ 455 g	6½ cups/ 910 g	13 cups/ 1,820 g
sea salt, fine grind	2 tsp/ 12 g	4 tsp/ 24 g	2 Tbsp plus 2 tsp/ 48 g
seed soaker, drained	all of it	all of it	all of it

Stir it up with your strong hands 'til it's good and mixed together (30 seconds to a minute will do). Cover and let it sit for 30 minutes to an hour, whatever is convenient. Go for a walk or read a book or talk to a friend.

6. Knead the dough. After it sits for a while, the dough is ready to be kneaded. Dip your hand in a bowl of water, then reach down into the side of the dough bowl, grab a little bit of it, and pull it up and push it down on top of the dough. Rotate the bowl a little bit and do it again. Be sweet and gentle yet firm with the dough. Do this to all of the dough; it'll probably take about ten folds. Cover the dough, and let it sit for ½ hour.

7. Stretch and fold a few more times. After ½ hour, stretch and fold the dough another ten times. Cover the dough, and leave it alone for another ½ hour or so. Do this another two times, at 15- to 30-minute intervals.

8. Choose your own path. Now you get to choose your own adventure for the **bulk rise.** Do what is convenient for you here.

If you want to shape your loaf in 2 to 3 hours, let the dough sit out somewhere in your kitchen.

If you want to shape your loaf anywhere from 12 to 48 hours later, stick it in the fridge (or just outside if it's cool out—about 45°F/7°C).

9. Pre-shape your loaf. After the dough has completed its bulk rise, lightly flour your counter and dump out the dough. Pre-shape your loaf, then let it rest for 10 to 15 minutes while you prepare to . . .

10. Coat it in sesame and poppy seeds. Wet a small towel, gently wring it out, and spread it out on a plate.

Take ½ cup/80 g of sesame seeds and ¼ cup/35 g of poppy seeds, mix them up, and spread them out on another plate.

Once your loaf has rested for 10 to 15 minutes after the pre-shape, do the final shape, then roll it in the wet towel to dampen it.

Now carefully roll your wet loaf in the bed of seeds, getting it completely covered.

Plop it into your UNFLOURED cloth-lined proofing basket, seam-side up.

11. Choose your own path. Now you get to choose your own adventure for the **final rise**. Again, do what is convenient for you here, folks!

If you want to bake bread in 3 to 4 hours, let the loaf sit out somewhere in your kitchen.

If you want to bake bread anywhere from 6 to 24 hours later, stick the loaf in the fridge (or just outside if it's cool out—about 45°F/7°C).

12. Preheat. Put your baking stone or Dutch oven on the middle rack of your oven and preheat to 475°F/240°C for 45 minutes.

13. Bake your bread. Sprinkle the loaf with cornmeal (or cover with parchment paper), and invert your loaf onto the large plate or pizza peel. (Or carefully plop the loaf into your preheated Dutch oven.) Slash the top with the razor, get it into the oven, and cover it with a pot or bowl (or the Dutch oven lid). Bake for 20 minutes, uncover, and get excited that your dough is magically turning into delicious bread. Bake for another 25 minutes. Check the bread and see how it's looking. If it's not dark brown, give it another 7 minutes.

14. Let it cool. Just take it nice and easy. You don't want to eat this bread before it's had ample time to cool down. If you rush it, the bread can actually have a gummy texture. Give it a couple of hours before you rip in.

Oh, man! Make this bread and eat it, quick!

WHAT YOU'LL NEED

FOODSTUFF	TOOLS
sourdough starter	measuring spoons
water	measuring cups
whole-wheat flour	thermometer (optional)
raisins, Thompson	big mixing bowl
cranberries, dried	mixing spoon
walnuts	2 plates or plastic wrap (for covering bowls)
sea salt, fine grind	small bowl or jar
rice flour	sharp knife
cornmeal (optional)	proofing basket and cloth
	spatula or bench knife
	baking stone and oven-safe pot or bowl (at least 6 in/15 cm tall and 12 in/31 cm wide) OR a Dutch oven
	parchment paper (optional)
	large plate or pizza peel
	double-edged razor blade with handle
	cooling rack (optional)

WHOLE-WHEAT CRANBERRY WALNUT

I first made this bread for Thanksgiving in 2010. I'd only been baking for a few months, so I didn't really know what I was doing, but many people told me it was their favorite. There's nothing too crazy about it; the combo of raisins, cranberries, and walnuts just meld beautifully with the hearty whole wheat.

1. Gather your foodstuff and tools.

2. **Make your sourdough pre-ferment.** Use starter that is sour smelling in a good way, most likely between 12 and 24 hours old. Make your pre-ferment 8 to 12 hours before you want to start mixing your

dough—likely in the evening before you go to bed or in the morning. You want it to be the consistency of thick pancake batter. Put this stuff in a big bowl:

	1 LOAF	2 LOAVES	4 LOAVES
sourdough starter	1 tsp/ 6 g	2 tsp/ 12 g	4 tsp/ 24 g
cool water (60°F/15°C)	¼ cup/ 60 g	½ cup/ 120 g	1 cup/ 240 g
whole-wheat flour	⅓ cup/ 50 g	⅔ cup/ 100 g	1⅓ cups/ 200 g

Mix it up real good. Cover with a plate or plastic wrap and leave it alone for 8 to 12 hours.

3. Make a cranberry and raisin soaker. Put the following in a small bowl or jar:

	1 LOAF	2 LOAVES	4 LOAVES
raisins, Thompson	¼ cup/ 35 g	½ cup/ 70 g	1 cup/ 140 g
cranberries, dried	¼ cup/ 35 g	½ cup/ 70 g	1 cup/ 140 g
hot water (100°F/38°C)	½ cup/ 120 g	1 cup/ 240 g	2 cups/ 480 g

Cover and set this stuff aside. (Drain the raisins and cranberries before adding them to your final dough.)

4. Prepare your walnuts. If you want to go the extra mile, toast the walnuts before adding them to your dough by spreading them out on a baking sheet and toasting them in a 400°F/200°C oven for 10 to 15 minutes, 'til they're a few shades darker than when you began and they smell heavenly. Let them cool for 15 minutes and coarsely chop those suckers with the sharp knife.

	1 LOAF	2 LOAVES	4 LOAVES
walnuts, toasted, coarsely chopped	⅓ cup/ 40 g	⅔ cup/ 80 g	1⅓ cups/ 160 g

5. Mix your dough. Uncover the big bowl, and take a big whiff. It should be putting off a pretty strong smell, nice and yummy, maybe a touch sour. If it doesn't, no biggie; it'll still make awesome bread. Add:

	1 LOAF	2 LOAVES	4 LOAVES
lukewarm water (80°F/27°C)	1½ cups/ 360 g	3 cups/ 720 g	6 cups/ 1,440 g
whole-wheat flour	3¼ cups/ 455 g	6½ cups/ 910 g	13 cups/ 1,820 g
sea salt, fine grind	2 tsp/ 12 g	4 tsp/ 24 g	2 Tbsp plus 2 tsp/ 48 g
toasted walnuts	all of them	all of them	all of them
cranberry and raisin soaker, drained	all of it	all of it	all of it

Stir it up with your strong hands 'til it's good and mixed together (30 seconds to a minute will do). Cover and let it sit for 30 minutes to an hour, whatever is convenient. Go for a walk or read a book or talk to a friend.

6. Knead the dough. After it sits for a while, the dough is ready to be kneaded. Dip your hand in a bowl of water, then reach down into the side of the dough bowl, grab a little bit of it, and pull it up and push it down on top of the dough. Rotate the bowl a little bit and do it again. Be sweet and gentle yet firm with the dough. Do this to all of the dough; it'll probably take about ten folds. Cover the dough, and let it sit for ½ hour.

7. Stretch and fold a few more times. After ½ hour, stretch and fold the dough another ten times. Cover the dough, and leave it alone for another ½ hour or so. Do this another two times, at 15- to 30-minute intervals.

8. Choose your own path. Now you get to choose your own adventure for the **bulk rise**. Do what is convenient for you here.

If you want to shape your loaf in 2 to 3 hours, let the dough sit out somewhere in your kitchen.

If you want to shape your loaf anywhere from 12 to 48 hours later, stick it in the fridge (or just outside if it's cool out—about 45°F/7°C).

9. Shape your loaf. After the dough has completed its bulk rise, flour your counter and dump out the dough. Pre-shape your loaf, then let it rest for 10 to 15 minutes. Shape it into a loaf and let it rest, seam-side down, while you line your proofing basket with a cloth that you've dusted with rice flour. Plop the loaf into the prepared proofing basket, seam-side up.

10. Choose your own path. Now you get to choose your own adventure for the **final rise**. Again, do what is convenient for you here, folks!

If you want to bake bread in 3 to 4 hours, let the loaf sit out somewhere in your kitchen.

If you want to bake bread anywhere from 6 to 24 hours later, stick the loaf in the fridge (or just outside if it's cool out—about 45°F/7°C).

11. Preheat. Put your baking stone or Dutch oven on the middle rack of your oven and preheat to 475°F/240°C for 45 minutes.

12. Bake your bread. Sprinkle the loaf with cornmeal (or cover with parchment paper), and invert your loaf onto the large plate or pizza peel. (Or carefully plop the loaf into your preheated Dutch oven.) Slash the top with the razor, get it into the oven, and cover it with a pot or bowl (or the Dutch oven lid). Bake for 20 minutes, uncover, and get excited that your dough is magically turning into delicious bread. Bake for another 25 minutes. Check the bread and see how it's looking. If it's not dark brown, give it another 7 minutes.

13. Let it cool. Whole-wheat bread really benefits from a little rest before you slice into it. Because it's such a wet dough, it can actually have a slightly gummy texture if it's not given proper time to mellow out after its bake. So just be patient, and give this loaf a couple of hours before tearing into it.

WHAT YOU'LL NEED

FOODSTUFF	TOOLS
sourdough starter	measuring spoons
water	measuring cups
whole-wheat flour	thermometer (optional)
raisins, Thompson	big mixing bowl
sea salt, fine grind	mixing spoon
cinnamon, ground	2 plates or plastic wrap (for covering bowls)
rice flour	small bowl or jar
cornmeal (optional)	proofing basket and cloth
	spatula or bench knife
	baking stone and oven-safe pot or bowl (at least 6 in/15 cm tall and 12 in/31 cm wide) OR a Dutch oven
	parchment paper (optional)
	large plate or pizza peel
	double-edged razor blade and handle
	cooling rack (optional)

WHOLE-WHEAT CINNAMON RAISIN

This is another really easy way to take your whole-wheat bread to a new and exciting place. Bake up a couple loaves of this, then treat yourself to some whole-wheat cinnamon raisin toast with butter and almond butter, and gift a loaf to a stranger walking down the street. You'll feel real good, I promise.

1. Gather your foodstuff and tools.

2. Make your sourdough pre-ferment. Use starter that is sour smelling in a good way, most likely between 12 and 24 hours old. Make your pre-ferment 8 to 12 hours before you want to start mixing your dough—likely in the evening before you go to bed or in the morning. You want it to be the consistency of thick pancake batter. Put this stuff in a big bowl:

	1 LOAF	2 LOAVES	4 LOAVES
sourdough starter	1 tsp/ 6 g	2 tsp/ 12 g	4 tsp/ 24 g
cool water (60°F/15°C)	¼ cup/ 60 g	½ cup/ 120 g	1 cup/ 240 g
whole-wheat flour	⅓ cup/ 50 g	⅔ cup/ 100 g	1⅓ cups/ 200 g

Mix it up real good. Cover with a plate or plastic wrap and leave it alone for 8 to 12 hours.

3. Make a raisin soaker. Put the following in a small bowl or jar:

	1 LOAF	2 LOAVES	4 LOAVES
raisins, Thompson	½ cup/ 70 g	1 cup/ 140 g	2 cups/ 280 g
hot water (100°F/38°C)	½ cup/ 120 g	1 cup/ 240 g	2 cups/ 480 g

Cover and set aside. (Drain the water from the raisins before adding them to your final dough.)

4. Mix your dough. Uncover the big bowl, and take a big whiff. It should be putting off a pretty strong smell, nice and yummy, maybe a touch sour. If it doesn't, no biggie; it'll still make awesome bread. Add:

	1 LOAF	2 LOAVES	4 LOAVES
lukewarm water (80°F/27°C)	1½ cups/ 360 g	3 cups/ 720 g	6 cups/ 1,440 g
whole-wheat flour	3¼ cups/ 455 g	6½ cups/ 910 g	13 cups/ 1,820 g
sea salt, fine grind	2 tsp/ 12 g	4 tsp/ 24 g	2 Tbsp plus 2 tsp/ 48 g
cinnamon, ground	2 tsp	4 tsp	2 Tbsp plus 2 tsp
raisin soaker, drained	all of it	all of it	all of it

Stir it up with your strong hands 'til it's good and mixed together (30 seconds to a minute will do). Cover and let it sit for 30 minutes to an hour, whatever is convenient. Go for a walk or read a book or talk to a friend.

5. Knead the dough. After it sits for a while, the dough is ready to be kneaded. Dip your hand in a bowl of water, then reach down into the side of the dough bowl, grab a little bit of it, and pull it up and push it down on top of the dough. Rotate the bowl a little bit and do it again. Be sweet and gentle yet firm with the dough. Do this to all of the dough; it'll probably take about ten folds. Cover the dough, and let sit for ½ hour.

6. Stretch and fold a few more times. After ½ hour, stretch and fold the dough another ten times. Cover the dough, and leave it alone for another ½ hour or so. Do this another two times, at 15- to 30-minute intervals.

7. Choose your own path. Now you get to choose your own adventure for the **bulk rise**. Do what is convenient for you here.

If you want to shape your loaf in 2 to 3 hours, let the dough sit out somewhere in your kitchen.

If you want to shape your loaf anywhere from 12 to 48 hours later, stick it in the fridge (or just outside if it's cool out—about 45°F/7°C).

8. Shape your loaf. After the dough has completed its bulk rise, flour your counter and dump out the dough. Pre-shape your loaf, then let it rest for 10 to 15 minutes. Shape it into a loaf and let it rest, seam-side down, while you line your proofing basket with a cloth that you've dusted with rice flour. Plop the loaf into the prepared proofing basket, seam-side up.

9. Choose your own path. Now you get to choose your own adventure for the **final rise**. Again, do what is convenient for you here, folks!

If you want to bake bread in 3 to 4 hours, let the loaf sit out somewhere in your kitchen.

If you want to bake bread anywhere from 6 to 24 hours later, stick the loaf in the fridge (or just outside if it's cool out—about 45°F/7°C).

10. Preheat. Put your baking stone or Dutch oven on the middle rack of your oven and preheat to 475°F/240°C for 45 minutes.

11. Bake your bread. Sprinkle the loaf with cornmeal (or cover with parchment paper), and invert your loaf onto the large plate or pizza peel. (Or carefully plop the loaf into your preheated Dutch oven.) Slash the top with the razor, get it into the oven, and cover it with a pot or bowl (or the Dutch oven lid). Bake for 20 minutes, uncover, and get excited that your dough is magically turning into delicious bread. Bake for another 25 minutes. Check the bread and see how it's looking. If it's not dark brown, give it another 7 minutes.

12. Let it cool. Whole-wheat bread really benefits from a little rest before you slice into it. Because it's such a wet dough, it can actually have a slightly gummy texture if it's not given proper time to mellow out after its bake. So just be patient, and give this loaf a couple of hours before tearing into it.

CHAPTER 5

ANOTHER NEW CHALLENGE / BREADS MADE FROM OTHER GRAINS

After a while with white flour, then with whole wheat, it was time to explore other grains. I'd grown a little bored, and I was also coming to realize that common wheat just didn't work out well for lots of people. So I wanted to experiment with other grains, and in the process maybe make some bread for folks with sensitivities to common wheat and/or gluten.

I started out with rye, and holy crap, I had no idea what I was in for. Rye does in fact have some gluten in it, but it's such a small amount that the dough never develops the ability to be stretched and tugged the way wheat dough does. It's just a slop the whole way through. For the first few months of my rye bread experiments, I baked loaves of bread that had reasonably good flavor, but the texture was waaaay off. It was always very gummy, not to mention that all of the loaves had a "flying roof."

I scoured the Internet and found a handful of anecdotes about the infamous "flying roof problem." A flying roof is a surefire way to ruin your day. Basically the loaf looks totally awesome from the outside, but when you cut into it you find a big hole right underneath the upper crust, and the inside of the loaf is often very dense and gooey. It's a big bummer, but again, you live and learn. I tried the solutions that everybody offered. Nothing worked—the flying roof was here to stay. And then one day it hit me: Ask Dave Miller. Who is Dave Miller? Well, that's gonna take a minute or two to explain.

I'd actually first heard of Dave Miller from a baker buddy back in Vermont, Adam of Bread & Butter Farm. I e-mailed Adam out of the blue one day and, just as I'd come to expect from fellow bread bakers, he graciously invited me to come on out and spend the day baking with him. Adam had a small bakery on his farm, and he was in love with rye. He'd spent some time in Germany, learning how to bake German-style rye breads, but he'd also spent some time with Dave. He spoke very highly of him, but at that point it was the first time I'd heard the name, so it didn't really stick.

After hearing about Dave from a handful of other baker buddies, I decided it was high time to meet the man behind the myth. Strangely enough, this revelation came while I was on an island in Thailand. I can't say exactly why, but I was surfing the Internet one morning in a café when I realized that I simply had to go visit him once I returned to America. A typically generous baker, Dave invited me to hang when I returned.

A week after I got back from Thailand I drove out to Yankee Hill, a tiny town about three hours northeast of San Francisco, to see what he was up to. What I found was one of the most inspiring bakers I'd ever met. He had a small bakery attached to his house, where he peacefully baked upward of 400 loaves, once a week, all by himself, all in a wood-fired oven, and he then sold the bread at the local farmers' market. Those are the facts, and they're rad enough, but the bread itself. . . .

Before getting in my car for the three-hour drive home, I ripped a small chunk off a loaf and put the rest in the trunk to keep me from eating too much. Of course, that didn't work—I pulled over three times in the first hour, each time to get another chunk of the unbelievable bread, still warm from the oven, bursting with flavors and textures I'd never imagined in a loaf of bread.

Dave does things very differently from most bakers. He makes whole-grain breads almost exclusively, and he mills all of his whole-grain flour himself, on a gorgeous mill that was made in Austria. Dave also buys his grains directly from farmers, paying way more than he has to, because he believes that the farmers should be paid a better wage for their hard work. Simply put, Dave is doing things in the most awesome way possible.

The following summer I was in need of a place to bake, and Dave was the first guy I thought of. Yes, it was over three hours away, but Dave was just such an inspiration and his bakery was so perfect, and he had that gorgeous mill that I was so eager to start practicing on (you'll see why in chapter 8). I asked him once, I asked him twice, and by the third time he said yes, I could come out and use his bakery on his off days. Dave's and my friendship had blossomed to the point where he accepted my repeated requests to use his bakery on his off days in order to bake my own bread. So I did just that for two months—made the three-hour drive to his bakery on Monday morning with a trunk full of

sourdough starter, then mixed, shaped, and baked 100 to 200 loaves of bread, making that three-hour drive back to San Francisco by Tuesday afternoon. It was incredible.

Anyway, Dave had some advice for my "flying roof" issue—oh, you know, just totally change the way I was treating the dough. Ya see, rye bread is a whole different beast than wheat bread, and it requires a different dance, which I most definitely did not know. I'd read things that hinted at this, but it took hearing the words from Dave's mouth for it to actually sink in. Lo and behold, I did what Dave said and the flying roof went away, never to return. (That's not totally true, but it makes a sweet story, eh?)

And my experiments didn't stop with rye. I started playing with other grains, like Kamut and spelt, and soon enough I'd developed a little repertoire of breads that, while being very similar to Dave's, were also my own. Here are a few of them for you to experiment with. May you never know the turmoil of the flying roof on your rye bread.

WHAT YOU'LL NEED

FOODSTUFF	TOOLS
sourdough starter	measuring spoons
water	measuring cups
Kamut flour	thermometer (optional)
sea salt, fine grind	big mixing bowl
	mixing spoon
	plate or plastic wrap (to cover bowl)
	oil or nonstick spray
	loaf pan (about 8 by 4 in/20 by 10 cm)
	aluminum foil
	cooling rack (optional)

KAMUT

I remember very clearly the first time I saw a 100 percent Kamut loaf, made with freshly milled Kamut flour, baked directly on the hearth. It emerged from the oven a supernatural combination of yellow, orange, red, and brown, with an ear you could slice a tomato on. In fact, it looked just like the picture on the facing page.

It had been made by the hands of Dave Miller, the master baker who so generously shared many an early morning with me, calmly shaping hundreds of loaves to perfection, then effortlessly loading and unloading them while I skipped around his bakery, jaw dropping in amazement, snapping hundreds of photos.

This dough can be tricky and weak, so I recommend that your first Kamut loaf be in a loaf pan.

If you're feeling bold, or if you've got the sandwich loaf under your belt, go all the way and do this one hearth style. Dave (and I) would be so proud of you.

↘ A very good question!

WHAT IN THE HECK IS "KAMUT"?
Kamut is a trademarked name that's used for a particular ancient variety of wheat, *khorasan*. In order for grain to be called Kamut, it has to meet a series of standards that were set by the company that owns the trademark. That's just a peek into the background of the name. Now, I can't speak to any scientific studies about this, but I hear that there are plenty of people who have trouble when they eat common wheat but who can eat the heck out of a loaf of Kamut bread and feel just

fine. Why might that be? Maybe because Kamut is an unadulterated ancient form of wheat that hasn't been genetically modified to be produced on a huge scale and to be resistant to all sorts of diseases. Or maybe because it has less gluten than common wheat, thereby not upsetting folks who have mild gluten sensitivities. Or maybe because it is usually milled as a whole-grain flour, and thereby used to make whole-grain bread. Or maybe it's just magic. I don't really know, but the bread tastes good, so just shut up and eat it.

1. Gather your foodstuff and tools.

2. Make your sourdough pre-ferment. Use starter that is sour smelling in a good way, most likely between 12 and 24 hours old. Make your sourdough pre-ferment 8 to 12 hours before you want to start mixing your dough. You're aiming to make it the consistency of thick pancake batter. Put this stuff in a big bowl:

	1 LOAF	2 LOAVES	4 LOAVES
sourdough starter	1 tsp/ 6 g	2 tsp/ 12 g	4 tsp/ 24 g
cool water (60°F/15°C)	¼ cup/ 60 g	½ cup/ 120 g	1 cup/ 240 g
Kamut flour	⅓ cup/ 50 g	⅔ cup/ 100 g	1⅓ cups/ 200 g

Mix it up real good. Cover with a plate or plastic wrap and leave it alone for 8 to 12 hours.

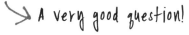

A very good question!

WHY AM I MAKING LESS SOURDOUGH PRE-FERMENT FOR THIS RECIPE?

Kamut dough ferments much faster than doughs that are made with white flour. Why? For the same reason that whole-wheat dough moves so quickly—Kamut flour is a whole-grain flour, and the microorganisms in

your sourdough starter just absolutely love it. I reduced the amount of sourdough pre-ferment in this recipe so that you can make it on the same schedule as the other recipes in this book. But if you want to speed things up, use more sourdough pre-ferment.

3. Mix the dough. Uncover the bowl of sourdough pre-ferment, and take a big whiff. It should be putting off a pretty strong smell, nice and yummy, maybe a touch sour. If it doesn't, no biggie; it'll still make awesome bread. Add:

	1 LOAF	2 LOAVES	4 LOAVES
lukewarm water (80°F/27°C)	1½ cups/ 360 g	3 cups/ 720 g	6 cups/ 1,440 g
Kamut flour	3½ cups/ 435 g	5 cups/ 870 g	10 cups/ 1,740 g
sea salt, fine grind	2 tsp/ 12 g	4 tsp/ 24 g	2 Tbsp plus 2 tsp/ 48 g

Stir it up with your strong hands 'til it's good and mixed together (30 seconds to a minute will do). Cover with a plate or plastic wrap, and let it sit for 30 minutes to an hour, whatever is convenient. Go for a walk or read a book or talk to a friend.

Isn't this dough beautiful? I LOVE the color, smell, and feel of Kamut dough, and I hope you do too.

4. Gently stretch and fold the dough. After it sits for a while, the dough is ready to be stretched and folded. Dip your hand in a bowl of water, then reach down into the side of the dough bowl, grab a little bit of it, and pull it up and push it down on top of the dough. This dough might tear a bit more than the other breads you've made, but it's all good; just keep up the good work. It'll come together after a few more stretches and folds. Rotate the bowl a little bit and do it again.

Be gentle with this dough; it's more fragile than dough made with common wheat flour. Do this to all of the dough; it'll probably take about ten folds. Cover the dough, and let it sit for ½ hour.

5. Stretch and fold a few more times. After ½ hour, stretch and fold the dough another ten times. Cover the dough, and leave it alone for another ½ hour or so. Do this another two times, at 15- to 30-minute intervals.

6. Choose your own path. Now you get to choose your own adventure for the **bulk rise**. Do what is convenient for you here.

If you want to shape your loaf in 2 to 3 hours, let the dough sit out somewhere in your kitchen.

If you want to shape your loaf anywhere from 12 to 48 hours later, stick it in the fridge (or just outside if it's cool out—about 45°F/7°C).

7. Shape your loaf. After the dough has completed its bulk rise, flour your counter and dump out the dough. Shape it into a log and plop it into a greased loaf pan, seam-side down. Cover with aluminum foil. See Lesson 2 for more details on this step.

8. Choose your own path. Now you get to choose your own adventure for the **final rise**. Again, do what is convenient for you here, folks!

If you want to bake bread in 2 to 3 hours, let the loaf sit out somewhere in your kitchen.

If you want to bake bread anywhere from 6 to 24 hours later, stick the loaf in the fridge (or just outside if it's cool out—45°F/7°C).

9. Preheat. Put one of the racks in the middle of your oven, and preheat to 475°F/240°C for 30 minutes. If you put the dough in the fridge, take it out while the oven is preheating so that it can warm up to room temperature before you bake it.

10. Bake your bread. Slide your loaf into the oven (with the aluminum foil still on top), and bake for 20 minutes. Then take off the foil, and revel at the loaf of bread you are making with this beautiful ancient grain. Bake for another 25 minutes. Check the bread to see how it's looking. If it's not dark brown, give it another 7 minutes.

11. Let it cool. Just like whole-wheat bread, Kamut bread really benefits from a little rest before you slice into it. Because it's such a wet dough, it can have a slightly gummy texture if it's not given proper time to mellow out after its bake. So just be patient, and give this loaf a couple of hours before tearing into it.

CORN KAMUT

One lucky summer I spent six hours a week in the car, driving out to bake in Dave Miller's bakery every Monday and Tuesday. The last time I went, I milled up a bunch of flour to bring back to San Francisco with me. But once I was back in SF, the flour just sat in its sack in my kitchen. I was intimidated by it! After a few weeks of this, I decided enough was enough: It was time for me to use this stuff. I wanted to make a bread with more than just Kamut flour in it, but what? I went poking around my kitchen and quickly found a nice fit— pumpkin seeds. What the heck, let's throw some of them in and see how it tastes. After a few flips through my bread cookbook library, I decided to add some cornmeal into the mix as well. Since the cornmeal and pumpkin seeds would weigh down this bread, I decided to blend it with some bread flour to lighten it up. I baked it up the next morning and shared it with my buddies Ian and Elicia, and they declared it a wild success. This one's for you, dudes.

If you're feeling bold, make this as a hearth loaf, but baking in a loaf pan is a much safer bet.

Follow the Kamut bread recipe (see page 127), with the following additions/changes:

When preparing your sourdough pre-ferment, also make a cornmeal and pumpkin seed soaker. Put the following in a bowl or jar:

	1 LOAF	2 LOAVES	4 LOAVES
cornmeal	¼ cup/ 40 g	½ cup/ 80 g	1 cup/ 160 g
pumpkin seeds	3 Tbsp/ 30 g	⅓ cup/ 55 g	¾ cup/ 120 g
boiling water	⅓ cup/ 80 g	⅔ cup/ 160 g	1⅓ cups/ 320 g

When mixing your dough in step 3, add all of the soaker together with the following to your sourdough pre-ferment:

	1 LOAF	2 LOAVES	4 LOAVES
lukewarm water (80°F/27°C)	1⅓ cups/ 320 g	2⅔ cups/ 640 g	5⅓ cups/ 1,280 g
Kamut flour	1 cup/ 145 g	2 cups/ 290 g	4 cups/ 580 g
bread flour	1½ cups/ 225 g	3 cups/ 450 g	6 cups/ 900 g
sea salt, fine grind	2 tsp/ 12 g	4 tsp/ 24 g	2 Tbsp plus 2 tsp/ 48 g

Follow the procedure in the Kamut bread recipe for mixing, rising, shaping, and baking.

When shaping your loaf, use cornmeal instead of flour on the counter, which will lead to a very nice and crunchy cornmeal crust.

WHAT YOU'LL NEED

FOODSTUFF	TOOLS
sourdough starter	measuring spoons
water	measuring cups
whole-spelt flour	thermometer (optional)
sea salt, fine grind	big mixing bowl
	mixing spoon
	plate or plastic wrap (to cover bowl)
	oil or nonstick spray
	loaf pan (about 8 by 4 in/20 by 10 cm)
	aluminum foil
	cooling rack (optional)

WHOLE SPELT

Spelt is another delicious ancient form of wheat. Some people who have trouble with common wheat can eat spelt; if this is you or someone you know, give this guy a try. Spelt makes a super-interesting dough, unlike any other I've ever worked with. When you first mix the flour with water, it feels very dry, as though you need more water. In fact, the first several times I made this bread I added too much water during the initial mix, ending up with a goopy dough that was pretty much impossible to work with. So don't add too much water! Once the dough comes together, it's amazing how you can stretch and stretch it, and it doesn't really pull back. This can take some getting used to, but once you've got the hang of it, whole spelt is an incredible bread to have in your repertoire.

Like Kamut dough, spelt dough can be tricky to work with, so I recommend that your first spelt loaf be in a loaf pan. If you're feeling bold, or if you've got the sandwich loaf under your belt, go all the way and do this one hearth style.

↳ A very good question!

WHAT IN THE HECK IS "SPELT"?

Spelt is an ancient variety of wheat. I can't speak to any scientific studies about this, but I hear that there are plenty of people who have trouble when they eat common wheat but can eat a loaf of spelt bread and feel just fine. Why might that be? It may be because it has less gluten than common wheat, thereby not upsetting folks who have mild gluten sensitivities. Or it may be because a lot of the time it's milled as a whole-grain flour. Or it may be the invisible spelt fairies, who take away all of your gastrointestinal issues. I'm not sure, but it is very yummy, so don't ask, and don't tell.

1. Gather your foodstuff and tools.

2. Make your sourdough pre-ferment. Use starter that is sour smelling in a good way, most likely between 12 and 24 hours old. Make your sourdough pre-ferment 8 to 12 hours before you want to start mixing your dough. (I usually do it either when I wake up or right before I go to bed.) You're aiming to make your sourdough pre-ferment the consistency of thick pancake batter. Put this stuff in a big bowl:

	1 LOAF	2 LOAVES	4 LOAVES
sourdough starter	1 tsp/ 6 g	2 tsp/ 12 g	4 tsp/ 24 g
cool water (60°F/15°C)	¼ cup/ 60 g	½ cup/ 120 g	1 cup/ 240 g
whole-spelt flour	½ cup/ 60 g	1 cup/ 120 g	2 cups/ 240 g

Mix it up real good. Cover with a plate or plastic wrap and leave it alone for 8 to 12 hours.

↘ A very good question!

WHY AM I MAKING LESS SOURDOUGH PRE-FERMENT FOR THIS RECIPE?

Spelt dough ferments much faster than doughs that are made with white flour. Why? For the same reason that whole-wheat dough moves so quickly—whole-spelt flour is a whole-grain flour, and the microorganisms in your sourdough starter just absolutely love it. I reduced the amount of sourdough pre-ferment in this recipe so that you can make it on the same schedule as the other recipes in this book. But if you want to speed things up, use more sourdough pre-ferment.

3. Mix the dough. Uncover the bowl of sourdough pre-ferment, and take a big whiff. It should be putting off a pretty strong smell, nice and yummy, maybe a touch sour. If it doesn't, no biggie; it'll still make awesome bread. Add:

	1 LOAF	2 LOAVES	4 LOAVES
lukewarm water (80°F/27°C)	1½ cups/ 360 g	3 cups/ 720 g	6 cups/ 1,440 g
whole-spelt flour	4 cups/ 480 g	8 cups/ 960 g	16 cups/ 1,920 g
sea salt, fine grind	2 tsp/ 12 g	4 tsp/ 24 g	2 Tbsp plus 2 tsp/ 48 g

Stir it up with your strong hands 'til it's good and mixed together (30 seconds to a minute will do). Cover with a plate or plastic wrap, and let it sit for 30 minutes to an hour, whatever is convenient. Go for a walk or read a book or talk to a friend.

Isn't this dough different from the other doughs? I LOVE the way you can *streeeeetch* it super-far, and it doesn't pull back. Fascinating.

4. Gently stretch and fold the dough. After it sits for a while, the dough is ready to be stretched and folded. Dip your hand in a bowl of water, then reach down into the side of the dough bowl, grab a little bit of it, and pull it up and push it down on top of the dough. This dough might tear a bit more than the other breads in this book, but it's all good; just keep up the good work, and be as gentle as you can. It'll come together after a few more stretches and folds. Rotate the bowl a little bit and do it again. Do this to all of the dough; it'll probably take about ten folds. Cover the dough, and let it sit for ½ hour.

5. Stretch and fold a few more times. After ½ hour, stretch and fold the dough another ten times. Cover the dough, and leave it alone for another ½ hour or so. Do this another two times, at 15- to 30-minute intervals.

6. Choose your own path. Now you get to choose your own adventure for the **bulk rise**. Do what is convenient for you here.

If you want to shape your loaf in 3 to 4 hours, let the dough sit out somewhere in your kitchen.

If you want to shape your loaf anywhere from 12 to 48 hours later, stick it in the fridge (or just outside if it's cool out—about 45°F/7°C).

7. Shape your loaf. After the dough has completed its bulk rise, flour your counter and dump out the dough. Shape it into a log, and plop it into a greased loaf pan, seam-side down. Spray or brush oil on the top of the loaf and cover with aluminum foil. See Lesson 2 for more details on this step.

8. Choose your own path. Now you get to choose your own adventure for the **final rise**. Again, do what is convenient for you here, folks!

If you want to bake bread in 3 to 4 hours, let the loaf sit out somewhere in your kitchen.

If you want to bake bread anywhere from 6 to 24 hours later, stick the loaf in the fridge (or just outside if it's cool out—about 45°F/7°C).

A very good question!

WHY DOES THE TOP OF MY SPELT LOAF LOOK FUNNY? WHAT ARE ALL THOSE BUBBLES?

A lot of the spelt loaves I have seen form bubbles on their surface in the time leading up to the bake. These were a bit unnerving to me at first, and I figured that I'd put too much water in my dough, and that the bread was going to turn out gross. But I was always pleasantly surprised when, after a spell in the oven, those unsightly bubbles were replaced by a beautiful brown crust and a moist and nutty crumb on the inside. My guess is that these bubbles form due to spelt's weak gluten. But don't let it worry you—your spelt loaf will grow up to be a normal bread, I promise.

9. Preheat. Put one of the racks in the middle of your oven, and preheat to 475°F/240°C for 30 minutes. If you put the dough in the fridge, take it out while the oven is preheating so that it can warm up to room temperature before you bake it.

10. Bake your bread. Slide your loaf into the oven (with the aluminum foil still on top), and bake for 20 minutes. Then take off the foil and revel at the loaf of bread you are making with this beautiful ancient grain. Bake for another 25 minutes. Check the bread to see how it's looking. If it's not dark brown, give it another 7 minutes.

11. Let it cool. Just like whole-wheat bread, spelt bread really benefits from a little rest before you slice into it. Because it's such a wet dough, it can have a slightly gummy texture if it's not given proper time to mellow out after its bake. So just be patient, and give this loaf a couple of hours before tearing into it.

FOODSTUFF	TOOLS
rolled oats	measuring cups or scale
sunflower seeds	measuring spoons
pumpkin seeds	big mixing bowl
almonds	oil or nonstick spray
flax seeds	loaf pan (about 8 by 4 in/20 by 10 cm)
psyllium seed husk	mixing spoons (optional)
chia seeds	cooling rack (optional)
sea salt, fine grind	
maple syrup	
olive oil	
water	

ADVENTURE BREAD

Sometimes you need a bread that is so dense, so hearty, so jam-packed full of seeds and grains (and devoid of air) that it will sustain you on your mightiest of adventures. That's what this bread is for. But that's not all it is for . . . it's also gluten-free! That will either entice you or turn you off, but either way I really hope that you give it a shot because it is incredible, and it is *suuuper* healthful. It's unlike any other bread in this book, in that there isn't even any flour in it, and it isn't fermented—it's basically just a bunch of seeds held together with a little bit of psyllium seed

husk and chia seeds. I started making it in the bakery because we kept having folks come in and ask us for gluten-free bread, and I got tired of saying no. Up until we made this bread, I had mostly been turned off by gluten-free breads, because it seemed like they were all just trying to imitate wheat breads, and failing miserably. But this bread stands on its own—it is gluten-free and proud of it. Special thanks goes out to Sarah Britton, blogger at My New Roots; her recipe inspired this bread.

yes, it's
gluten-free!

1. Gather your foodstuff and tools.

2. Toast the seeds. Preheat your oven to 350°F/180°C. Spread the sunflower and pumpkin seeds on a baking sheet and toast until they start to brown, about 15 minutes, stirring halfway through baking.

3. Measure ingredients. Dump this stuff into a big bowl:

	1 LOAF	2 LOAVES	4 LOAVES
rolled oats	2¼ cups/ 235 g	4½ cups/ 470 g	9 cups/ 940 g
sunflower seeds	1 cup/ 160 g	2 cups/ 320 g	4 cups/ 640 g
pumpkin seeds	½ cup/ 65 g	1 cup/ 130 g	2 cups/ 260 g
almonds, toasted and coarsely chopped (see page 114)	¾ cup/ 90 g	1½ cups/ 180 g	3 cups/ 360 g
flax seeds	¾ cup/ 120 g	1½ cups/ 240 g	3 cups/ 480 g
psyllium seed husk	⅓ cup/ 25 g	⅔ cup/ 50 g	1⅓ cups/ 100 g
chia seeds	3 Tbsp/ 25 g	6 Tbsp/ 50 g	¾ cup/ 100 g
sea salt, fine grind	2 tsp/ 12 g	4 tsp/ 24 g	2 Tbsp plus 2 tsp/48 g

Then pour in all the wet stuff:

maple syrup	2 Tbsp/ 40 g	¼ cup/ 80 g	½ cup/ 160 g
olive oil	¼ cup/ 55 g	½ cup/ 110 g	1 cup/ 220 g
water	2½ cups/ 600 g	5 cups/ 1,200 g	10 cups/ 2,400 g

4. Mix it all up, scoop into pan. Oil your loaf pan, and then mush up your "dough" real good with your strong hands or a big spoon. Take pride in your mush-job, this is all of the handling you're going to do with this "dough." Once it's mixed real good, scoop it into your oiled pan and smooth out the top so it looks nice. Then stick that guy in the fridge and leave it alone for at least a few hours, or up to a whole day.

5. Bake it. Put a rack in the middle of the oven and preheat to 400°F/200°C. Bake for about an hour or so, then take it out and gently remove the loaf from the pan. Let it cool on a cooling rack for at least 2 hours (YES, two whole hours). Don't rush it here folks, this bread is D-E-N-S-E, and if you don't wait for it to cool, it really won't be as yummy.

6. Toast and eat. This bread is definitely best sliced nice and thin (around ½ in/12 mm) and then toasted up and spread with whatever your heart desires. And don't worry, if you're adventuring somewhere without toaster access (like a gorgeous river in the middle of nowhere), it will still be scrumptious, I promise.

WHAT YOU'LL NEED

FOODSTUFF	TOOLS
sunflower seeds	measuring cups
sesame seeds	small bowl or jar
flax seeds	2 plates or plastic wrap (to cover bowls)
cornmeal	measuring spoons
water	thermometer (optional)
sourdough starter	big mixing bowl
whole-rye flour	mixing spoon (optional)
sea salt, fine grind	oil or nonstick spray
	loaf pan (about 8 by 4 in/20 by 10 cm)
	spatula or bench knife
	aluminum foil
	cooling rack

DARK MOUNTAIN RYE

Ever since I fell in love with baking, I'd been fascinated by this particular type of bread, with the name that I didn't totally know how to say, *Vollkornbrot*. It sounded so magical, like a tiny unknown village in the forest where elves and pixies dance in the moonlight. Apparently it is a traditional German style of bread, made from 100 percent coarsely ground rye berries (no wheat flour) and leavened with a sourdough starter, and it is said to keep for weeks. It took me over a year to finally take a stab at making it, and it took me months to get it right, but I eventually got there. Now it's my favorite bread, and I'm not the only one—for a while *Rafi refused to eat*

any other bread. I knew I'd landed on something special, and now I take immense joy in sharing it with you. I named it "dark mountain rye" because it's the type of bread that you should take into the mountains with you—it will sustain you on your most righteous adventures.

A few words of warning. This bread requires a totally different treatment from all of the other breads in this book. Rye ferments much faster than wheat, and you can't even cut into the bread until it's rested for a day after baking. All of this is worth it; just make it and see for yourself.

A very good question!

WHAT IS RYE?

Rye is another type of grain, similar to wheat in some ways and very different in others. It can make a very delicious loaf of bread, but it will never make bread that is as light and fluffy as wheat bread, because it doesn't contain enough gluten. Gluten is that special protein in wheat that allows dough to form a matrix of gas-trapping pockets, which turn your dense blob of dough into a light and holey loaf. Before rye berries are ground into flour, they look similar to wheat berries, though usually they have more of a gray-green hue to them. They can be ground into very fine flour, or they can be just broken into a very coarse meal. Pumpernickel flour is a coarsely ground flour, with visible chunks of rye berries still intact. It's actually possible to make "white rye flour" as well, which, like white wheat flour, is just made from the interior, starch-rich portion of the rye berry, removing the nutrient-rich bran and germ. This recipe includes whole-rye flour—plain and simple, it's the entire rye berry, ground up into flour.

1. Gather your foodstuff and tools.

2. Toast the seeds. Preheat your oven to 350°F/180°C. Spread all the seeds on a baking sheet and toast until they start to brown, about 15 minutes, stirring halfway through baking.

3. Make your seed soaker. This bread's heavy on the seeds, and seeds are thirsty, so make this guy when you make your sourdough pre-ferment. Put the following in a small bowl or jar:

	1 LOAF	2 LOAVES	4 LOAVES
sunflower seeds	½ cup/ 80 g	1 cup/ 160 g	2 cups/ 320 g
sesame seeds	½ cup/ 80 g	1 cup/ 160 g	2 cups/ 320 g
flax seeds	¼ cup/ 40 g	½ cup/ 80 g	1 cup/ 160 g
cornmeal	¼ cup/ 40 g	½ cup/ 80 g	1 cup/ 160 g
hot water (as hot as your tap can get)	1 cup/ 240 g	2 cups/ 280 g	4 cups/ 960 g

Cover and set aside. (Drain the water from the seeds before adding them to your final dough.)

4. Make your sourdough pre-ferment. Use starter that is sour smelling in a good way, most likely between 12 and 24 hours old. Make your sourdough pre-ferment 12 to 14 hours before you want to start mixing your dough. You're aiming to make your sourdough pre-ferment the consistency of thick paste. Put this stuff in a big bowl:

	1 LOAF	2 LOAVES	4 LOAVES
sourdough starter	1 tsp/ 6 g	2 tsp/ 12 g	4 tsp/ 24 g
cool water (60°F/15°C)	¼ cup/ 60 g	½ cup/ 120 g	1 cup/ 240 g
whole-rye flour	½ cup/ 70 g	1 cup/ 140 g	1¾ cups/ 245 g

Mix it up real good. Cover with a plate or plastic wrap, and leave it alone for 12 hours. Take a peek and see if it's grown. If it hasn't expanded at all, wait another few hours, then forge ahead.

5. Mix the dough. Uncover the bowl of sourdough pre-ferment, and take a big whiff. It should be putting off a pretty strong smell, a bit more sour than the other breads in this book. Add:

	1 LOAF	2 LOAVES	4 LOAVES
lukewarm water (80°F/27°C)	1⅓ cups/ 320 g	2⅔ cups/ 640 g	5⅓ cups/ 1,280 g
whole-rye flour	3½ cups/ 490 g	7 cups/ 980 g	14 cups/ 1,960 g
sea salt, fine grind	2½ tsp/ 15 g	1 Tbsp plus 2 tsp/ 30 g	3 Tbsp plus 1 tsp/ 60 g
seed soaker, drained	all of it	all of it	all of it

Stir it up with a big spoon, or your hands if you're ready to get super-messy. This dough feels very different from any of the other breads you've been making. Cover with a plate or plastic wrap, and let it sit for 90 minutes. YES—only AN HOUR AND A HALF. Rye ferments quickly.

6. Scoop that slop. Roll up your sleeves, because you're about to get messy. This dough is a paste, and it requires scooping. Wet your hand and scoop the dough into a greased loaf pan. Use a wet spatula, bench knife, or your fingers to smooth the top of the dough, once it's all in the pan. Sprinkle some cornmeal on top and feel good about yourself. Then use a spatula to make five to seven ½-in/12-mm deep cuts diagonally across the loaf (see bottom-right photo, facing page). Cover with oiled aluminum foil.

7. Let it rise. This bread rises for a shorter time than the other breads—only 1½ to 2 hours. You should see some cracks start to form on the top of the bread, but even if you don't, worry not. The real magic will happen in the oven.

8. Preheat. Put one of the racks in the middle of your oven, and preheat to 400°F/200°C for 30 minutes.

9. Bake your bread. Slide your loaf into the oven (with the aluminum foil still on top), and bake for 30 minutes. Then take off the foil, turn the heat down to 300°F/150°C, and bake for another hour. Take that sucker outta there, remove it from the pan, and let it cool on a rack.

10. Let the loaf rest for a day. This is really going to take some patience, but you've gotta take my word for it—the bread isn't finished baking yet. You can try to open it up now, but I promise you—it will be gummy and weird tasting, and you will think that you've failed. Rye bread is just a totally different beast, and it requires time to develop. So seriously—set the loaf somewhere in your kitchen where you won't be tempted, and just let it be for 24 hours. It'll be worth it.

CHAPTER 6

BAKING ON THE SIDE (OR IN THE BACKYARD) / PIZZA

When I was a kid I hated tomato sauce, and would eat only white Hawaiian pizza. No sauce (revolting)—just cheese, ham, and pineapple. And man, I would scarf that Hawaiian pizza with a vengeance. By high school I'd warmed up to the joys of tomatoes on my pie, and I found a job in a little pizza joint called HomeBake Pizza Shoppe. It was the perfect high school job—roll over to the pizza shop where I "worked" with my buddies, blaring Bob Dylan and Bob Marley, unsupervised by adults, making pizza all night long. The shop was called HomeBake, for god's sake. I'm sure you can figure out the rest.

My time at HomeBake planted the seeds for a serious love affair with the pizza pie that began a decade later. I was at a friend's backyard party when I saw something I'd never imagined before—a small wood-fired pizza oven on top of a barbecue grill. I immediately approached the guy who was manning it and offered myself up for assistance. He seemed open to my help, so I spent the next several hours with my face jammed in the oven, inhaling an endless stream of smoke, obsessed with what I was doing, helping to bake the best pizza I'd ever eaten.

His name was Jeff Krupman, but his working name was The PizzaHacker. Over the next several months I baked pizza with him a few times a week, gleaning lots of tips and tricks he'd discovered during his pizza obsession. Jeff did things right—he hand-mixed all of his sourdough pizza dough, he made his own tomato sauce from locally grown tomatoes, he properly seasoned his pies (meaning he put on enough salt), and, of course, he baked them in an 800°F/425°C wood-fired oven that he had designed and built himself. All of these things came together to make incredible pizza.

A few months later I was at another party (come on, you know you like to party too) when I met an extremely excitable and wide-eyed man. His name was Charlie, and I'd actually heard a lot about him, as my friend who was dating him thought that we were going to get along really well. He'd recently fallen in love with bread baking, and so within minutes we were gushing about the joys of sourdough bread, trading tips about maintaining our starters, and just generally having ourselves a very nice time. I told him that I'd been baking and selling bread out of my home oven but was on the hunt for a bigger oven to do my thing. Without hesitation he invited me to come and bake bread in the wood-fired oven in his Italian restaurant in Oakland, Pizzaiolo.

The next week I showed up at Pizzaiolo with a few tubs of dough, a backpack full of proofing baskets, and a very vague idea of what I was about to do. Charlie set me up on a bench in the back of the restaurant, and I set to work shaping loaves. I finished up a couple hours later, rolled the rack of proofing loaves into the walk-in, and went to Charlie's house to sleep for a few hours. The next morning we arrived at the restaurant before any of the cooks had shown up and loaded the dough into the oven. As staff shuffled in, there was a palpable excitement in the air. Folks had heard that there was a new bread baker coming in, and they were excited to try the bread. As the minutes passed I grew anxious—my preparation for this bake had come from a few hours spent reading online. At about the 20-minute mark I decided it was time to check on the bread. Everyone was surprised by what we found.

A large plume of smoke puffed out of the oven, and this was followed by me unloading thirty black, inedible "loaves of bread." Good lord. Luckily, Charlie proved to be one of the most generous guys around—he invited me to continue baking in and learning to use his oven, and once I had it down, he started serving my bread in the restaurant. I did this once or twice a week for a year—baking bread for Pizzaiolo, but also baking bread for my bread subscription customers. I developed a loyal following, and some of my fondest bread memories are of late nights and early mornings at Pizzaiolo. I still burnt a loaf of bread every now and then, but by the end of my time there I'd learned how to tame that wild beast of a wood-fired oven.

By the next fall, I'd built a wood-fired oven of my own in my backyard, and it was integral to many a raucous pizza party.

PIZZA
BREAD MAKER
SINCE 2010

WHAT YOU'LL NEED

FOODSTUFF	TOOLS
sourdough starter	measuring spoons
water	measuring cups
whole-wheat flour	thermometer (optional)
bread flour	big mixing bowl
sea salt, fine grind	mixing spoon
cherry tomatoes (or your favorite tomato sauce)	plate (optional)
	plastic wrap
fresh basil	baking pan (optional)
fresh mozzarella cheese	sharp knife
extra-virgin olive oil	large broiler-safe frying pan with flaring sides (at least 12 in/31 cm wide)
smoked sea salt	
	fork or spatula
Parmesan cheese	cutting board
	grater
	pizza cutter (optional)

THE RADDEST HOMEMADE PIZZA THE WORLD HAS EVER KNOWN

The baking method I'm about to teach you is one of those things that I wish I'd learned as a child (or as a teenager, really), because I'm telling you—it makes the best homemade pizza I've ever had. The reason this method works so well is that it allows you to blast the pizza dough with the most heat possible from a home oven, in a really controlled way. How does this happen, you so eagerly ask? Nope, it's not with a baking stone in the broiler—it's a double bake! First on the stovetop, then in the broiler. Crazy, right? I learned this method from San Francisco pizza guru The PizzaHacker. He makes a living baking and selling pizzas out of a wood-fired pizza oven that he built on a Weber grill. He would most definitely not accept credit for this method (because he is just such a lovely and modest fellow), but he was the one who taught me, so I'm citing him. Many thanks, Krup.

Do me a favor and make this basic pizza recipe before trying the other ones. There are a few tips and tricks and details that I include here, and leave out of the other ones, that will make your pizza as good as it can be.

1. Gather your foodstuff and tools.

2. Make your sourdough pre-ferment. Use starter that is sour smelling in a good way, most likely between 12 and 24 hours old. Make your pre-ferment 8 to 12 hours before you want to start mixing your dough—likely in the evening before you go to bed or in the morning. You want it to be the consistency of thick pancake batter. Put this stuff in a big bowl:

	4 PIZZAS	8 PIZZAS	16 PIZZAS
sourdough starter	1 Tbsp/ 15 g	2 Tbsp/ 30 g	¼ cup/ 60 g
cool water (60°F/15°C)	½ cup/ 120 g	1 cup/ 240 g	2 cups/ 480 g
whole-wheat flour	¾ cup/ 105 g	1½ cups/ 210 g	3 cups/ 420 g

Mix it up real good. Cover with a plate or plastic wrap and leave it alone for 8 to 12 hours.

3. Mix the dough. Mix into your sourdough pre-ferment:

	4 PIZZAS	8 PIZZAS	16 PIZZAS
lukewarm water (80°F/27°C)	1 cup/ 240 g	2 cups/ 480 g	4 cups/ 960 g
bread flour	2¾ cups/ 415 g	5½ cups/ 830 g	11 cups/ 1,660 g
sea salt, fine grind	2 tsp/ 12 g	4 tsp/ 24 g	2 Tbsp plus 2 tsp/ 48 g

This dough will be a little more difficult to mix than the bread dough you've been making, as it includes a little more flour, resulting in a stiffer dough. Don't be scared; just proceed as normal, and everything will be fine. Once you've mixed everything, cover your bowl with a plate or plastic wrap, and let it sit for 30 minutes to an hour.

↘ A very good question!

THIS IS VERY SIMILAR TO THE BREAD DOUGH I'VE BEEN MAKING—WHAT'S UP?
Indeed, if you're paying super-close attention, you will notice that this dough is almost exactly the same, just a little bit stiffer (more flour) than the bread dough you've been making. Using a touch more flour will lead to a pizza dough that's essentially stronger, making it much easier to shape into a pizza and also yielding a crisper crust.

4. Knead the dough. After the dough sits for a while, stretch and fold it as you've done a million times before (refer to page 61 for a refresher). This dough will be a little stiffer than the bread dough, but just stay strong, and remember—be sweet and gentle yet firm. Once you're done, cover the dough, and let it sit for ½ hour.

5. Knead a few more times. After ½ hour, stretch and fold the dough another ten times. Cover the dough, and leave it alone for another ½ hour or so. Do this another two times, at 15- to 30-minute intervals.

6. Choose your own path. Now you get to choose your own adventure for the **bulk rise**. Do what is convenient for you here.

If you want to shape your dough into balls in 3 to 4 hours, let it sit out somewhere in your kitchen.

If you want to shape your dough into balls anywhere from 12 to 48 hours later, stick it in the fridge (or just outside if it's cool out—about 45°F/7°C).

7. Shape the dough into balls. After the dough has completed its bulk rise, flour your counter and dump out the dough. Cut off a piece of dough about 8 oz/225 g—it'll make a ball that's about 3 in/7.5 cm in diameter. Use a little flour on your hands to shape it into a ball, and set it on a plate or in a baking pan, seam-side down. Do this with all of the dough, placing the balls next to one another.

If you want to bake pizza within a couple of hours, cover the dough with plastic wrap and leave it on the countertop.

If you want to bake in 6 to 24 hours, cover the dough with plastic wrap or a plastic bag, leave it at room temperature for an hour, and then put it in the refrigerator. If you do this, you'll need to let the dough warm up for 30 to 45 minutes when you're ready to make pizza.

8. Prepare the toppings. We're going simple with this pie: tomato, basil, and cheese (and salt). Cherry tomatoes are delicious and easy to find, but if you have a favorite tomato sauce then be my guest—you'll need about ¼ cup/70 g of sauce per pie.

	4 PIZZAS	8 PIZZAS	16 PIZZAS
cherry tomatoes	2 pints/ 680 g	4 pints/ 1,360 g	8 pints/ 2,720 g
fresh basil	20 to 25 big leaves	45 to 50 big leaves	90 to 100 big leaves
fresh mozzarella cheese	10 oz/ 320 g	20 oz/ 640 g	40 oz/ 1,280 g

Slice each cherry tomato in half, or it will burst when it bakes. Rip the basil leaves off their stems.

9. Preheat the frying pan and broiler. Once you're ready to make pizza, put your frying pan on the stovetop, pour in 1 Tbsp of olive oil, and turn that burner on high. Turn on the broiler as well, and position a rack as close to the broiler as you can. It will take 6 to 8 minutes for both of these to get screaming hot, and you'll know the pan is ready when the oil is smoking. Just open your windows and get pumped.

10. Stretch the dough and toss it in the pan. Toss a tablespoon's worth of flour on your countertop, and plop a dough ball onto it. Sprinkle a little bit more flour on top of the dough, and get to work gently stretching it into a round shape.

Use your fingertips to press the dough ball into a circle.

Lift up the dough and gently squeeze it between your fingers and thumb, creating a lip around the outer edge.

Lay the dough down on the counter, and hit it with a little more flour to prevent sticking.

Pick up the dough, lay it across the backs of your hands, and gently stretch it out to 10 to 12 in/25 to 31 cm in diameter. Once it's as big as the frying pan, toss it in there.

11. Build the pie. You've got about 3 minutes until the bottom is baked, so there's no need to rush this. You can do it however you want, but I like this way:

- Sprinkle about **1 tsp of smoked sea salt** on the pizza, mostly on the outer edge of the crust.

- Spread **1 cup/170 g of sliced cherry tomatoes** (or ¼ cup/70 g of sauce) out to within about 1½ in/4 cm of the outer edge.

- Artfully toss on **5 or 6 big basil leaves**, distributing evenly.

• Rip up **2½ oz/80 g of fresh mozzarella** into five or six pieces, and toss them on the pie, covering each basil leaf so the leaves don't burn.

Once you're done, use a fork or spatula to lift up the dough, and check the color of the bottom. When it has some dark brown spots, it is ready to go in the broiler.

12. Pop it in the broiler. Use an oven mitt or towel to place the frying pan in the broiler. It will probably take 2 to 3 minutes to get nice and speckled, brown with some specks of black. Check it after a minute, and rotate the pan if it's browning unevenly.

13. Take it out, and finish the pie. Be careful taking it out of the broiler, as everything is hot as hell. Slide your pizza out of the frying pan and onto a cutting board. Drizzle the pie with some extra-virgin olive oil and grate some Parmesan cheese on it. Cut it up into slices, let it cool for a minute, and share it with someone you have a crush on.

BAKER'S PERCENTAGE

Bread flour	79%
Whole-wheat flour	21%
Water	68%
Salt	2.3%

this is the big bread
oven at my bakery.
Look at those cute
little loaves!

WHAT YOU'LL NEED

FOODSTUFF	TOOLS
sourdough starter	measuring spoons
water	measuring cups
whole-wheat flour	thermometer (optional)
bread flour	big mixing bowl
sea salt, fine grind	mixing spoon
figs (preferably fresh, but dried is fine)	plate (optional)
	plastic wrap
Gorgonzola (or other stinky cheese)	baking pan (optional)
rosemary (preferably fresh)	sharp knife
fresh mozzarella cheese	large broiler-safe frying pan with flaring sides (at least 12 in/31 cm wide)
smoked sea salt	pastry brush or spoon
extra-virgin olive oil	fork or spatula
	cutting board
	pizza cutter (optional)

FIG, GORGONZOLA, AND ROSEMARY (CROWD PLEASER)

This is a combination I learned from The PizzaHacker. Pizza purists will scoff at this pie, but I don't give a damn—it's incredible. If you're lucky enough to have some fresh figs at your disposal, then please, oh please, use them on this pizza. Otherwise, dried figs will do the trick just fine. If blue cheese isn't your thing, feel free to try something a little milder.

Just so ya know—you're gonna do almost everything the same as the original pizza recipe, except for the toppings.

1. Gather your foodstuff and tools.

2. Make your sourdough pre-ferment. Use starter that is sour smelling in a good way, most likely between 12 and 24 hours old. Make your pre-ferment 8 to 12 hours before you want to start mixing your dough—likely in the evening before you go to bed or in the morning. You want it to be the consistency of thick pancake batter. Put this stuff in a big bowl:

	4 PIZZAS	8 PIZZAS	16 PIZZAS
sourdough starter	1 Tbsp/ 15 g	2 Tbsp/ 30 g	¼ cup/ 60 g
cool water (60°F/15°C)	½ cup/ 120 g	1 cup/ 240 g	2 cups/ 480 g
whole-wheat flour	¾ cup/ 105 g	1½ cups/ 210 g	3 cups/ 420 g

Mix it up real good. Cover with a plate or plastic wrap and leave it alone for 8 to 12 hours.

3. **Mix the dough.** Mix into your sourdough pre-ferment:

	4 PIZZAS	8 PIZZAS	16 PIZZAS
lukewarm water (80°F/27°C)	1 cup/ 240 g	2 cups/ 480 g	4 cups/ 960 g
bread flour	2¾ cups/ 415 g	5½ cups/ 830 g	11 cups/ 1,660 g
sea salt, fine grind	2 tsp/ 12 g	4 tsp/ 24 g	2 Tbsp plus 2 tsp/ 48 g

This dough will be a little more difficult to mix than the bread dough you've been making, as it includes a little less water, resulting in a stiffer dough. Don't be scared; just proceed as normal, and everything will be fine. Once you've mixed everything, cover your bowl with a plate or plastic wrap, and let it sit for 30 minutes to an hour.

4. **Knead the dough.** After the dough sits for a while, stretch and fold it as you've done a million times before (refer to page 61 for a refresher). This dough will be a little stiffer than the bread dough, but just stay strong, and remember—be sweet and gentle yet firm. Once you're done, cover the dough, and let it sit for ½ hour.

5. **Stretch and fold a few more times.** After ½ hour, stretch and fold the dough another ten times. Cover the dough, and leave it alone for another ½ hour or so. Do this another two times, at 15- to 30-minute intervals.

6. **Choose your own path.** Now you get to choose your own adventure for the **bulk rise**. Do what is convenient for you here.

If you want to shape your dough into balls in 3 to 4 hours, let the dough sit out somewhere in your kitchen.

If you want to shape your dough into balls anywhere from 12 to 48 hours later, stick it in the fridge (or just outside if it's cool out—about 45°F/7°C).

7. **Shape the dough into balls.** After the dough has completed its bulk rise, flour your counter and dump out the dough. Cut off a piece of dough about 8 oz/ 225 g—it'll make a ball that's about 3 in/7.5 cm in diameter. Use a little flour on your hands to shape it into a ball, and set it on a plate or in a baking pan, seam-side down. Do this with all of the dough.

If you want to bake pizza within a couple of hours, cover the dough with plastic wrap and leave it on the countertop.

If you want to bake in 6 to 24 hours, cover the dough with plastic wrap or a plastic bag, leave it at room temperature for an hour, and then put it in the refrigerator.

8. Prepare the toppings. You've got it pretty easy on this one:

	4 PIZZAS	8 PIZZAS	16 PIZZAS
figs, coarsely chopped	1 cup/ 150 g	2 cups/ 300 g	4 cups/ 600 g
Gorgonzola, crumbled	1 cup/ 140 g	2 cups/ 280g	4 cups/ 560 g
rosemary, chopped	3 Tbsp/ 6 g fresh or 2 tsp dried	6 Tbsp/ 12 g fresh or 4 tsp dried	¾ cup/ 24 g fresh or 2 Tbsp plus 2 tsp dried
fresh mozzarella cheese	10 oz/ 320 g	20 oz/ 640 g	40 oz/ 1,280 g

Yes, all ya gotta do is coarsely chop the figs and chop up the rosemary and BLAMMO, you're almost ready to please a crowd.

9. Preheat the frying pan and broiler. Once you're ready to make pizza, put your frying pan on the stovetop, pour in 1 Tbsp of olive oil, and turn that burner on high. Turn on the broiler as well. Wait 6 to 8 minutes for both of these to get screaming hot. You'll know the pan is ready when the oil is smoking. Open your windows and get pumped.

10. Stretch the dough and toss it in the pan. Toss a tablespoon's worth of flour on your countertop, and plop a dough ball onto it. Sprinkle a little bit more flour on top of the dough, and get to work gently stretching it into a round shape. Use your fingertips to press the dough ball into a circle, then lift up the dough and gently squeeze it between your fingers and thumb, creating a lip around the outer edge. Lay the dough down on the counter, and hit it with a little more flour to prevent sticking. Then pick up the dough, lay it across the backs of your hands, and gently stretch it out to 10 to 12 in/ 25 to 31 cm in diameter. Once it's as big as the frying pan, toss it in there.

check the bottom.

sprinkle on salt.

11. Build the pie. You've got about 3 minutes until the bottom is baked, so there's no need to rush this. You can do it however you want, but I like this way:

- Sprinkle about **1 tsp of smoked sea salt** on the pizza, mostly on the outer edge of the crust.

- Pour **2 to 3 Tbsp of extra-virgin olive oil** on the pizza, using a pastry brush or spoon to spread it evenly out to within about 1½ in/4 cm of the outer edge.

- Spread **¼ cup/35 g of coarsely chopped figs** onto the pie, distributing them evenly.

- Sprinkle **¼ cup/35 g of crumbled Gorgonzola** on the pie, taking care to not have any clumps that are larger than a nickel. (Too much blue cheese seriously grosses me out.)

- Artfully toss on your **rosemary—2 tsp if using fresh** or ½ tsp if it's dried.

- Rip up **½ cup/80 g of fresh mozzarella** into five or six pieces, and toss them on the pie.

Once you're done, use a fork or spatula to lift up the dough, and check the color of the bottom. When it has some dark brown spots, it is ready to go in the broiler.

12. Pop it in the broiler. Use an oven mitt or towel to place the frying pan in the broiler. It will probably take 2 to 3 minutes to get nice and speckled, brown with some specks of black. Check it after a minute, and rotate the pan if it's browning unevenly.

13. Take it out, and finish the pie. Be careful taking it out of the broiler, as everything is hot as hell. Slide your pizza out of the frying pan and onto a cutting board. Drizzle the pie with some extra-virgin olive oil and sprinkle with smoked salt. Cut it up into slices, let it cool for a minute, and share it with someone you have a crush on.

on go the figs . . .

and goooooood cheese.

WHAT YOU'LL NEED

FOODSTUFF	TOOLS
sourdough starter	measuring spoons
water	measuring cups
whole-wheat flour	thermometer (optional)
bread flour	big mixing bowl
sea salt, fine grind	mixing spoon
green olives (or other type)	plate (optional)
fontina cheese	plastic wrap
russet potatoes (or other type)	baking pan (optional)
thyme, preferably fresh	sharp knife
fresh mozzarella cheese	mandoline (optional)
extra-virgin olive oil	large broiler-safe frying pan with flaring sides (at least 12 in/31 cm wide)
smoked sea salt	pastry brush or spoon
Parmesan cheese (optional)	fork or spatula
	cutting board
	grater (optional)
	pizza cutter (optional)

POTATO, OLIVE, AND FONTINA

I think the first time I had this pizza was at Charlie Hallowell's incredible Oakland restaurant, Pizzaiolo. I liked it so much that I ordered it every week for months. The salty olives with the creamy fontina were a wonderful balance, and the potatoes lent a familiarity that made me feel nice and easy every time I got a bite in my mouth. I prefer to use green olives for this one, but you could just as easily use another variety. Same thing with the potatoes—I like russet, but follow your fancy.

Just so ya know—you're gonna do everything the same as the original pizza recipe, except for the toppings.

1. Gather your foodstuff and tools.

2. **Make your sourdough pre-ferment.** Use starter that is sour smelling in a good way, most likely between 12 and 24 hours old. Make your pre-ferment 8 to 12 hours before you want to start mixing your

dough—likely in the evening before you go to bed or in the morning. You want it to be the consistency of thick pancake batter. Put this stuff in a big bowl:

	4 PIZZAS	8 PIZZAS	16 PIZZAS
sourdough starter	1 Tbsp/ 15 g	2 Tbsp/ 30 g	¼ cup/ 60 g
cool water (60°F/15°C)	½ cup/ 120 g	1 cup/ 240 g	2 cups/ 480 g
whole-wheat flour	¾ cup/ 105 g	1½ cups/ 210 g	3 cups/ 420 g

Mix it up real good. Cover with a plate or plastic wrap and leave it alone for 8 to 12 hours.

3. Mix the dough. Mix the following into your sourdough pre-ferment:

	4 PIZZAS	8 PIZZAS	16 PIZZAS
lukewarm water (80°F/27°C)	1 cup/ 240 g	2 cups/ 480 g	4 cups/ 960 g
bread flour	2¾ cups/ 415 g	5½ cups/ 830 g	11 cups/ 1,660 g
sea salt, fine grind	2 tsp/ 12 g	4 tsp/ 24 g	2 Tbsp plus 2 tsp/ 48 g

This dough will be a little more difficult to mix than the bread dough you've been making, as it includes a little less water, resulting in a stiffer dough. Don't be scared; just proceed as normal, and everything will be fine. Once you've mixed everything, cover your bowl with a plate or plastic wrap, and let it sit for 30 minutes to an hour.

4. Knead the dough. After the dough sits for a while, stretch and fold it as you've done a million times before (refer to page 61 for a refresher). This dough will be a little stiffer than the bread dough, but just stay strong, and remember—be sweet and gentle yet firm. Once you're done, cover the dough, and let it sit for ½ hour.

5. Stretch and fold a few more times. After ½ hour, stretch and fold the dough another ten times. Cover the dough, and leave it alone for another ½ hour or so. Do this another two times, at 15- to 30-minute intervals.

6. Choose your own path. Now you get to choose your own adventure for the **bulk rise.** Do what is convenient for you here.

If you want to shape your dough into balls in 3 to 4 hours, let the dough sit out somewhere in your kitchen.

If you want to shape your dough into balls anywhere from 12 to 48 hours later, stick it in the fridge (or just outside if it's cool out—about 45°F/7°C).

7. Shape the dough into balls. After the dough has completed its bulk rise, flour your counter and dump out the dough. Cut off a piece of dough about 8 oz/ 225 g—it'll make a ball that's about 3 in/7.5 cm in diameter. Use a little flour on your hands to shape it into a ball, and set it on a plate or in a baking pan, seam-side down. Do this with all of the dough.

If you want to bake pizza within a couple of hours, cover the dough with plastic wrap and leave on the countertop.

If you want to bake in 6 to 24 hours, cover the dough with plastic wrap or a plastic bag, leave it at room temperature for an hour, and then put it in the refrigerator.

8. Prepare the toppings. Pit and coarsely chop those olives. If you have a mandoline, use it for the fontina and potatoes; otherwise just slice them both up into the thinnest slices you can manage.

	4 PIZZAS	8 PIZZAS	16 PIZZAS
olives, pitted and coarsely chopped	2 cups/ 560 g	4 cups/ 1,120 g	8 cups/ 2,240 g
fontina cheese	1 cup/ 150 g	2 cups/ 300 g	4 cups/ 600 g
potatoes	2 medium	4 medium	8 medium
thyme	3 Tbsp/ 6 g fresh or 2 tsp dried	6 Tbsp/ 12 g fresh or 4 tsp dried	¾ cup/ 24 g fresh or 2 Tbsp plus 2 tsp dried
fresh mozzarella cheese	2 cups/ 320 g	4 cups/ 640 g	8 cups/ 1,280 g

9. Preheat the frying pan and broiler. Once you're ready to make pizza, put your frying pan on the stovetop, pour in 1 Tbsp of olive oil, and turn that burner on high. Turn on the broiler as well. Wait 6 to 8 minutes for both of these to get screaming hot. You'll know the pan is ready when the oil is smoking. Open your windows and get pumped.

10. Stretch the dough and toss it in the pan. Toss a tablespoon's worth of flour on your countertop, and plop a dough ball onto it. Sprinkle a little bit more flour on top of the dough, and get to work gently stretching it into a round shape. Use your fingertips to press the dough ball into a circle, then lift up the dough and gently squeeze it between your fingers and thumb, creating a lip around the outer edge. Lay the dough down on the counter, and hit it with a little more flour to prevent sticking. Then pick up the dough, lay it across the backs of your hands, and gently stretch it out to 10 to 12 in/25 to 31 cm in diameter. Once it's as big as the frying pan, toss it in there.

11. Build the pie. You've got about 3 minutes until the bottom is baked, so there's no need to rush this. You can do it however you want, but I like this way:

- Sprinkle about **1 tsp of smoked sea salt** on the pizza, mostly on the outer edge of the crust.

- Pour **2 to 3 Tbsp of extra-virgin olive oil** on the pizza, using a pastry brush or spoon to spread it evenly out to within about 1½ in/4 cm of the outer edge.

- Spread **½ cup/70 g of coarsely chopped olives** onto the pie, distributing them evenly.

- Spread **half of a potato in slices** on the pie, distributing evenly.

- Toss on **¼ cup/40 g of thinly sliced fontina cheese.**

- Sprinkle with your **thyme**—2 tsp if using fresh or ½ tsp if it's dried.

- Rip up **½ cup/80 g of fresh mozzarella** into five or six pieces, and toss them on the pie.

Once you're done, use a fork or spatula to lift up the dough, and check the color of the bottom. When it has some dark brown spots, it is ready to go in the broiler.

12. Pop it in the broiler. Use an oven mitt or towel to place the frying pan in the broiler. It will probably take 2 to 3 minutes to get nice and speckled, brown with some specks of black. Check it after a minute, and rotate the pan if it's browning unevenly.

13. Take it out, and finish the pie. Be careful taking it out of the broiler, as everything is hot as hell. Slide your pizza out of the frying pan and onto a cutting board.

Optional bonus move: *Drizzle 1 to 2 Tbsp of extra-virgin olive oil onto the pie, and grate some Parmesan cheese on top as well.*

Cut it up into slices, let it cool for a minute, and eat the whole thing yourself.

WHAT YOU'LL NEED

FOODSTUFF	TOOLS
sourdough starter	measuring spoons
water	measuring cups
whole-wheat flour	thermometer (optional)
bread flour	big mixing bowl
sea salt, fine grind	mixing spoon
thick-cut bacon	plate (optional)
Cheddar cheese	plastic wrap
eggs	baking pan (optional)
smoked sea salt	sharp knife
extra-virgin olive oil	grater
Parmesan cheese (optional)	large broiler-safe frying pan with flaring sides (at least 12 in/31 cm wide)
	pastry brush or spoon
	fork or spatula
	cutting board
	pizza cutter (optional)

BACON, EGG, AND CHEESE (BREAKFAST PIE)

Who says pizza isn't a good breakfast food? It's true that most people don't do pizza for breakfast (unless they're in college and the pizza is cold), but this pie is an amazing way to start the day and will make for a brunch party that goes down in history. The addition of a fresh egg in the middle of this pizza is an elegant touch; just be sure to bake it properly—not too much, not too little—so you can drizzle the yolk over the entire pie hot outta the broiler.

You're gonna do everything the same as the original pizza recipe, except for the toppings.

1. Gather your foodstuff and tools.

2. Make your sourdough pre-ferment. Use starter that is sour smelling in a good way, most likely between 12 and 24 hours old. Make your pre-ferment 8 to 12 hours before you want to start mixing your dough—likely in the evening before you go to bed or in the morning. You want it to be the consistency of thick pancake batter. Put this stuff in a big bowl:

	4 PIZZAS	8 PIZZAS	16 PIZZAS
sourdough starter	1 Tbsp/ 15 g	2 Tbsp/ 30 g	¼ cup/ 60 g
cool water (60°F/15°C)	½ cup/ 120 g	1 cup/ 240 g	2 cups/ 480 g
whole-wheat flour	¾ cup/ 105 g	1½ cups/ 210 g	3 cups/ 420 g

Mix it up real good. Cover with a plate or plastic wrap and leave it alone for 8 to 12 hours.

3. Mix the dough. Mix the following into your sourdough pre-ferment:

	4 PIZZAS	8 PIZZAS	16 PIZZAS
lukewarm water (80°F/27°C)	1 cup/ 240 g	2 cups/ 480 g	4 cups/ 960 g
bread flour	2¾ cups/ 415 g	5½ cups/ 830 g	11 cups/ 1,660 g
sea salt, fine grind	2 tsp/ 12 g	4 tsp/ 24 g	2 Tbsp plus 2 tsp/ 48 g

This dough will be a little more difficult to mix than the bread dough you've been making, as it includes a little less water, resulting in a stiffer dough. Don't be scared; just proceed as normal, and everything will be fine. Once you've mixed everything, cover your bowl with a plate or plastic wrap, and let it sit for 30 minutes to an hour.

4. Knead the dough. After the dough sits for a while, stretch and fold it as you've done a million times before (refer to page 61 for a refresher). This dough will be a little stiffer than the bread dough, but just stay strong, and remember—be sweet and gentle yet firm. Once you're done, cover the dough, and let sit for ½ hour.

5. Stretch and fold a few more times. After ½ hour, stretch and fold the dough another ten times. Cover the dough, and leave it alone for another ½ hour or so. Do this another two times, at 15- to 30-minute intervals.

6. Choose your own path. Now you get to choose your own adventure for the **bulk rise.** Do what is convenient for you here.

If you want to shape your dough into balls in 3 to 4 hours, let the dough sit out somewhere in your kitchen.

If you want to shape your dough into balls anywhere from 12 to 48 hours later, stick it in the fridge (or just outside if it's cool out—about 45°F/7°C).

7. Shape the dough into balls. After the dough has completed its bulk rise, flour your counter and dump out the dough. Cut off a piece of dough about 8 oz/ 225 g—it'll make a ball that's about 3 in/7.5 cm in diameter. Use a little flour on your hands to shape it into a ball, and set it on a plate or in a baking pan, seam-side down. Do this with all of the dough.

If you want to bake pizza within a couple of hours, cover the dough with plastic wrap and leave it on the countertop.

If you want to bake in 6 to 24 hours, cover the dough with plastic wrap or a plastic bag, leave it at room temperature for an hour, and then put it in the refrigerator.

8. Prepare the toppings. Coarsely chop the bacon, but don't worry about precooking—it'll cook while the pizza bakes. As for the Cheddar cheese, grate it up. Get those eggs, but leave them raw—we're going to bake them while they're on the pie.

	4 PIZZAS	8 PIZZAS	16 PIZZAS
thick-cut bacon, coarsely chopped	8 slices/ 180 g	16 slices/ 360 g	32 slices/ 720 g
Cheddar cheese, grated	1 cup/ 120 g	2 cups/ 240 g	4 cups/ 480 g
eggs	4 large	8 large	16 large

9. Preheat the frying pan and broiler. Once you're ready to make pizza, put your frying pan on the stovetop, add 1 Tbsp of olive oil, and turn that burner up as high as it will go. Turn on the broiler as well. Wait 6 to 8 minutes for both of these to get screaming hot.

10. Stretch the dough and toss it in the pan. Toss a tablespoon's worth of flour on your countertop, and plop a dough ball onto it. Sprinkle a little bit more flour on top of the dough, and get to work gently stretching it into a round shape. Use your fingertips to press the dough ball into a circle, then lift up the dough and gently squeeze it between your fingers and thumb, creating a lip around the outer edge. Lay the dough down on the counter, and hit it with a little more flour to prevent sticking. Then pick up the dough, lay it across the backs of your hands, and gently stretch it out to 10 to 12 in/ 25 to 31 cm in diameter. Once it's as big as the frying pan, toss it in there.

11. Build the pie. You've got about 3 minutes until the bottom is baked, so no need to rush this. You can do it however you want, but I like this way:

- Sprinkle about **1 tsp of smoked sea salt** on the pizza, mostly on the outer edge of the crust.

- Pour **2 to 3 Tbsp of extra-virgin olive oil** on the pizza, using a pastry brush or spoon to spread it evenly out to within about 1½ in/4 cm of the outer edge.

- Spread **¼ cup/45 g of bacon pieces** onto the pie, distributing them evenly.

- Toss on **¼ cup/30 g of grated Cheddar cheese.**

- Carefully **crack an egg** right into the middle of that sucker.

Once you're done, use a fork or spatula to lift up the dough, and check the color of the bottom. When it has some dark brown spots, it is ready to go in the broiler.

12. Pop it in the broiler. Use an oven mitt or towel to place the frying pan in the broiler. It will probably take 2 to 3 minutes to get nice and speckled, brown with some specks of black. The egg should firm up slightly but still be runny—you're aiming for a sunny-side-up consistency. Check it after a minute, and rotate the pan if it's browning unevenly.

13. Take it out, and finish the pie. Be careful taking it out of the broiler, as everything is hot as hell. Slide your pizza out of the frying pan and onto a cutting board. Grate some Parmesan cheese on top, if you like, then cut the pie tic-tac-toe style and use a spoon to drizzle the yolk over the entire pizza.

Don't stop here

Listen dudes, you can put whatever the heck you want on your pizza. That's part of the fun of pizza at home, right? So don't be shy; there are a million different possibilities here—get crazy.

CHAPTER 7

WAIT A SECOND, I'M A . . . BAKER? / POCKETBREADS

Baking at Pizzaiolo was incredible, but it was also pretty inconvenient. I had to mix my dough elsewhere, bring it to the restaurant at night, sleep over at Charlie's, then get up at 3 A.M. and bake and be all done by 7 A.M. I knew that if I wanted to take things to the next level I would have to find a place to bake closer to home, where I could settle in a bit more. I was still pushing the limits of my home oven—after months of tweaking, I maxed out at twelve hearth loaves per bake. It was time to find a bigger oven.

I was nowhere near ready to open my own bakery, but I figured that perhaps I could find a bakery that would let me bake in their oven when they weren't using it. I wandered around the neighborhood, asking any bakery I passed if they were interested in renting me some time and space. Most people were confused by my request, and none of them were interested. But this all changed one day when I wandered into Mission Pie, an adorable bakery and café in the Mission District of San Francisco.

First I met Krystin, one of the owners. I gave her a loaf of my olive bread and told her about what I'd been doing at home, selling my bread by subscription to folks around the neighborhood. Might she have any interest in letting me bake my bread at Mission Pie, and bring it around the city on my bike? She liked the idea of my Community Supported Bread but wasn't super-keen on the idea of me coming in, baking a bunch of bread, and then taking all of it away. Furthermore, it wasn't something she or her partner Karen had ever done at

Mission Pie, nor were they eager to start—renting time and space to someone who, while being very passionate, didn't have much of an idea about what he was doing. She'd think about it.

A couple weeks later I swung back through with another loaf of bread, and this time I sat down with Krystin and Karen, and we were able to come up with a nice idea. I could try baking there one day a week as long as I (1) brought all of my supplies with me when I showed up, (2) took them away when I was done, and (3) baked a handful of loaves to sell to Mission Pie's walk-in customers.

Amazing!!! Now I just needed to figure out how to use that oven. . . .

So I just started doing it. I'd bring in all of my stuff in a backpack and some buckets: flour, seeds, proofing baskets, tiny digital scale. This was my only choice, as I was still baking at home and at Pizzaiolo on other days, so I had to bring my stuff with me wherever I went. After a month of this, I asked if I could maybe have a tiny space in the basement to leave some things between bakes. Karen and Krystin kindly obliged and let me start using a broken refrigerator as my storage unit.

After baking and selling bread at Mission Pie for a few months, I had a new problem—if I was going to turn this bread-baking thing into my job for real, I had to figure out how to make it a little more profitable. In this vein, I realized a pattern with customers, a conversation that went something like this:

me: <excitedly> Wanna try some bread I just baked?

Customer: <surprised, but enticed> Oh my—I didn't realize you sold bread here! Sure, I'll try some. <takes bread, eats it, furrows brow, and gets excited> Whoa, this is delicious!

me: Aww, really? Thank you! That's my whole wheat, but I've also got a sourdough sandwich loaf and a walnut bread.

Customer: Those sound great, but I can't eat a whole loaf myself. Do you have anything smaller?

me: Uhh, no, just these loaves here.

Customer: Well that's stupid. You should, because then I could buy something from you.

me: Thanks for the advice. <sheepishly> But you didn't have to call me stupid.

Customer: <aggressively> What did you just say?

me: Nothing! Have a great day! Byeeeeee!

(I made up that last part about my customer calling me stupid. That never happened, not once.)

Thus, pocketbreads were born.

The premise of the pocketbread was to take dough that I was already mixing and turn it into something smaller that folks could buy who weren't looking for the commitment of an entire loaf. So I started taking 10 to 15 pounds of my bread dough, tossing stuff in, shaping it into tiny loaves, and seeing how people liked them. It turned out that people liked the ones with sweet stuff in them, like chocolate. I tried a bunch of different shapes before I settled on using muffin tins.

And the name—how did I come up with that? My genius roommates Brendan and Lana dreamed it up one day. It was logical to them—bread that can fit in your pocket = pocketbreads. Very cute, very clever.

Pocketbreads were a big deal for my budding bread business. Some days I sold seventy-five of those little suckers, at $2 a pop. This was big for me at the time, scraping by as I was. It meant another couple hundred bucks a week, and it meant that I could keep diving deeper into bread.

So deeper into bread I dove.

WHAT YOU'LL NEED

FOODSTUFF	TOOLS
Bing cherries, pitted and dried (or fresh if they're in season)	sharp knife
	measuring cups
water	small bowl or jar
sourdough starter	2 plates or plastic wrap (to cover bowls)
whole-wheat flour	
bread flour	thermometer (optional)
sea salt, fine grind	measuring spoons
dark chocolate bar(s)	big mixing bowl
cornmeal	mixing spoon
	vegetable oil or nonstick spray
	muffin tins
	small towel
	large plastic bag, such as a clean garbage bag
	double-edged razor blade and handle
	spray bottle
	cooling rack (optional)

DARK CHOCOLATE CHERRY

This was the first pocketbread I made that had people coming back for more. I had two wonderful customers, a husband and wife, who would pick up a dozen of these little treats before going on long flights (she was a flight attendant). They'd actually get upset with me when I didn't make them. Well, this one's for you two.

Aside from the addition of dark chocolate and cherries in this recipe (and the shaping, of course), everything is very similar to the free-form hearth sourdough loaf (Lesson 6).

1. Gather your foodstuff and tools.

2. Make your cherry soaker. Coarsely chop up the dried cherries. Put them in a small bowl or jar with the hot water and cover so that water can't evaporate. No need to make a soaker if you're using fresh cherries; they can get mixed into the dough as is. But pit them before chopping. (Drain the soaked cherries before using.)

	12 POCKET-BREADS	24 POCKET-BREADS	48 POCKET-BREADS
dried cherries, chopped	½ cup/ 90 g	1 cup/ 180 g	2 cups/ 360 g
hot water (100°F/ 38°C)	½ cup/ 120 g	1 cup/ 240 g	2 cups/ 480 g

	12 POCKET-BREADS	24 POCKET-BREADS	48 POCKET-BREADS
lukewarm water (80°F/27°C)	1¼ cups/ 300 g	2½ cups/ 600 g	5 cups/ 1,200 g
bread flour	3 cups/ 450 g	6 cups/ 900 g	12 cups/ 1,800 g
sea salt, fine grind	2 tsp/ 12 g	4 tsp/ 24 g	2 Tbsp plus 2 tsp/ 48 g
cherry soaker, drained	all of it	all of it	all of it
dark chocolate, coarsely chopped	¼ cup/ 45 g	½ cup/ 90 g	1 cup/ 180 g

3. Make your sourdough pre-ferment. Use starter that is sour smelling in a good way, most likely between 12 and 24 hours old. Make your pre-ferment 8 to 12 hours before you want to start mixing your dough—likely in the evening before you go to bed or in the morning. You want it to be the consistency of thick pancake batter. Put this stuff in a big bowl:

	12 POCKET-BREADS	24 POCKET-BREADS	48 POCKET-BREADS
sourdough starter	1 Tbsp/ 15 g	2 Tbsp/ 30 g	¼ cup/ 60 g
cool water (60°F/15°C)	½ cup/ 120 g	1 cup/ 240 g	2 cups/ 480 g
whole-wheat flour	¾ cup/ 105 g	1½ cups/ 210 g	3 cups/ 420 g

Mix it up real good. Cover with a plate or plastic wrap and leave it alone for 8 to 12 hours.

4. Mix the dough. Uncover the bowl of sourdough pre-ferment, and take a big whiff. It should be putting off a pretty strong smell, nice and yummy, maybe a touch sour. Add:

Mix everything together so that it's evenly combined, just for 30 seconds to a minute. Cover with a plate or plastic wrap, and let it sit for 30 minutes to an hour, whatever is convenient.

5. Gently stretch and fold the dough. Dip your hand in a bowl of water, then reach down into the side of the dough bowl, grab a little bit of it, and pull it up and push it down on top of the dough. Rotate the bowl a little bit and do it again to another portion of the dough. Give the dough about ten stretches and folds. Cover the dough, and let it sit for ½ hour.

6. Stretch and fold a few more times. After ½ hour, stretch and fold the dough another ten times. Cover the dough, and leave it alone for another ½ hour or so. Do this another two times, at 15- to 30-minute intervals.

7. Choose your own path. Choose your own adventure for the **bulk rise.**

If you want to shape your pocketbreads in 3 to 4 hours, let the dough sit out somewhere in your kitchen.

If you want to shape your pocketbreads anywhere from 12 to 48 hours later, stick it in the fridge (or just outside if it's cool out—about 45°F/7°C).

8. Shape your pocketbreads. After the dough has completed its bulk rise, flour your counter and dump out the dough. Cut the dough into ¾ cup/100-g pieces (to fill up your muffin tin about two-thirds of the way), and use a little bit of flour on your hands to shape them into round balls. Let them rest on your counter while you prepare to cover them in cornmeal.

9. Grease your muffin tin. Use vegetable oil or nonstick spray to coat the individual cups.

10. Cover them in cornmeal. To give each pocketbread a cornmeal crust, do this:

Wet a small towel, gently wring it out, and spread it out on a plate.

Take ½ cup/80 g of cornmeal, and spread it out on another plate.

Gently lift up a pocketbread, and roll it in the wet towel to dampen it.

Now carefully roll your wet pocketbread in the bed of cornmeal, being sure to get it completely covered. Plop the pocketbread into your muffin tin, seam-side down. When you're all done, put the filled muffin tin in a plastic bag, so that the tops don't dry out. (A CLEAN garbage bag works great for this.)

11. Choose your own path. Choose your own adventure for the **final rise.**

If you want to bake your pocketbreads in 3 to 4 hours, let them sit out somewhere in your kitchen.

If you want to bake them anywhere from 6 to 24 hours later, put them in the fridge (or just outside if it's cool out—about 45°F/7°C).

12. Preheat. Once your pocketbreads have risen, preheat your oven to 475°F/240°C for 20 minutes. If you put the pocketbreads in the fridge, take them out while the oven is preheating so that they can warm up to room temperature before you bake them.

13. Bake your pocketbreads. Take the pans out of the bag, slash the top of each pocketbread with a razor, spray their tops with water, using a spray bottle, and get them in the oven. Bake for 5 minutes, then quickly open the oven, spray them again, and just as quickly close the oven. Bake for another 25 minutes, and check on them. You'll know they are done when the slashed portions are good and dark brown.

14. Once they're baked, take them out of the pan and let them cool on a cooling rack.

WHAT YOU'LL NEED

FOODSTUFF	TOOLS
fennel seeds	electric spice grinder or mortar and pestle
golden raisins	measuring spoons
cornmeal	measuring cups
water	thermometer (optional)
sourdough starter	small bowl or jar
whole-wheat flour	big mixing bowl
bread flour	mixing spoon
sea salt, fine grind	2 plates or plastic wrap (to cover bowls)
	vegetable oil or nonstick spray
	muffin tins
	small towel
	large plastic bag, such as a clean garbage bag
	double-edged razor blade and handle
	spray bottle
	cooling rack

GOLDEN RAISIN AND FENNEL

I first ate this combo—golden raisins, fennel seed, and cornmeal—at a bakery in New York, Amy's Bread. I had one bite, and I knew that I had to figure out my own version. After a few attempts I was very close, but something was lacking—the cornmeal crust! I covered these little beauties in cornmeal and never looked back. They quickly became one of my faves (and I'm not alone, as I soon learned), and I hope they do the same for you.

Aside from the addition of golden raisins, fennel seeds, and cornmeal in this recipe (and the shaping, of course), everything is very similar to the hearth sourdough (Lesson 6).

1. Gather your foodstuff and tools.

2. Make your raisin soaker. Grind the fennel seeds right before adding them to this soaker, with an electric spice grinder or a good old-fashioned mortar and pestle. Measure and mix in a small bowl or jar:

	12 POCKET-BREADS	24 POCKET-BREADS	48 POCKET-BREADS
fennel seeds, ground	2 tsp	1 Tbsp plus 1 tsp	2 Tbsp plus 2 tsp
golden raisins	½ cup/ 70 g	1 cup/ 140 g	2 cups/ 280 g
cornmeal	¼ cup/ 40 g	½ cup/ 80 g	1 cup/ 160 g
hot water (100°F/ 38°C)	½ cup/ 120 g	1 cup/ 240 g	2 cups/ 480 g

Mix everything together and cover it, so the water can't evaporate, and set aside. (Drain before using.)

3. Make your sourdough pre-ferment. Use starter that is sour smelling in a good way, most likely between 12 and 24 hours old. Make your pre-ferment 8 to 12 hours before you want to start mixing your dough—likely in the evening before you go to bed or in the morning. You want it to be the consistency of thick pancake batter. Put this stuff in a big bowl:

	12 POCKET-BREADS	24 POCKET-BREADS	48 POCKET-BREADS
sourdough starter	1 Tbsp/ 15 g	2 Tbsp/ 30 g	¼ cup/ 60 g
cool water (60°F/15°C)	½ cup/ 120 g	1 cup/ 240 g	2 cups/ 480 g
whole-wheat flour	¾ cup/ 105 g	1½ cups/ 210 g	3 cups/ 420 g

Mix it up real good. Cover with a plate or plastic wrap and leave it alone for 8 to 12 hours.

4. Mix the dough. Uncover the bowl of sourdough pre-ferment, and take a big whiff. It should be putting off a pretty strong smell, nice and yummy, maybe a touch sour. Add:

	12 POCKET-BREADS	24 POCKET-BREADS	48 POCKET-BREADS
lukewarm water (80°F/27°C)	1¼ cups/ 300 g	2½ cups/ 600 g	5 cups/ 1,200 g
bread flour	3 cups/ 450 g	6 cups/ 900 g	12 cups/ 1,800 g
sea salt, fine grind	2 tsp/ 12 g	4 tsp/ 24 g	2 Tbsp plus 2 tsp/ 48 g
raisin soaker, drained	all of it	all of it	all of it

Mix everything together so that it's evenly combined, just for 30 seconds to a minute. Cover with a plate or plastic wrap, and let it sit for 30 minutes to an hour, whatever is convenient.

5. Gently stretch and fold the dough. Dip your hand in a bowl of water, then reach down into the side of the dough bowl, grab a little bit of it, and pull it up and push it down on top of the dough. Rotate the bowl a little bit and do it again to another portion of the dough. Give the dough about ten stretches and folds. Cover the dough, and let it sit for ½ hour.

6. Stretch and fold a few more times. After ½ hour, stretch and fold the dough another ten times. Cover the dough, and leave it alone for another ½ hour or so. Do this another two times, at 15- to 30-minute intervals.

7. Choose your own path. Choose your own adventure for the **bulk rise.**

If you want to shape your pocketbreads in 3 to 4 hours, let the dough sit out somewhere in your kitchen.

If you want to shape your pocketbreads anywhere from 12 to 48 hours later, stick it in the fridge (or just outside if it's cool out—about 45°F/7°C).

8. Shape your pocketbreads. After the dough has completed its bulk rise, flour your counter, and dump out the dough. Cut the dough into ¾-cup/100-g pieces (to fill up your muffin tin about two-thirds of the way), and use a little bit of flour on your hands to shape them into round balls. Let them rest on your counter while you prepare to cover them in cornmeal.

9. Grease your muffin tin. Use vegetable oil or nonstick spray to coat the individual cups.

10. Cover them in cornmeal. To give each pocketbread a cornmeal crust, do this:

Wet a small towel, gently wring it out, and spread it out on a plate.

Take ½ cup/80 g of cornmeal, and spread it out on another plate.

Gently lift up a pocketbread, and roll it in the wet towel to dampen it.

Now carefully roll your wet pocketbread in the bed of cornmeal, being sure to get it completely covered. Plop the pocketbread into your muffin tin, seam-side down. When you're all done, put the muffin tin in a plastic bag, so that the tops don't dry out. (A CLEAN garbage bag works great for this.)

11. Choose your own path. Choose your own adventure for the final rise.

If you want to bake your pocketbreads in 3 to 4 hours, let them sit out somewhere in your kitchen.

If you want to bake them anywhere from 6 to 24 hours later, put them in the fridge (or just outside if it's cool out—about 45°F/7°C).

12. Preheat. Once your pocketbreads have risen, preheat your oven to 450°F/230°C for 20 minutes. If you put the pocketbreads in the fridge, take them out while the oven is preheating so that they can warm up to room temperature before you bake them.

13. Bake your pocketbreads. Take the pans out of the bag, slash the top of each pocketbread with a razor, spray their tops with water, using a spray bottle, and get them in the oven. Bake for 5 minutes, then quickly open the oven, spray them again, and just as quickly close the oven. Bake for another 25 minutes, and check on them. You'll know they are done when the slashed portions are good and dark brown.

14. Once they're baked, take them out of the pan and let them cool on a cooling rack.

you know you wanna
make this bread . . .
just do it, baker!

WHAT YOU'LL NEED

FOODSTUFF	TOOLS
sourdough starter	measuring spoons
water	measuring cups
whole-wheat flour	thermometer (optional)
chocolate peanut butter cups	big mixing bowl
bread flour	mixing spoon
sea salt, fine grind	plate or plastic wrap (to cover bowl)
	sharp knife
	vegetable oil or nonstick spray
	muffin tins
	large plastic bag (such as a clean garbage bag)
	double-edged razor blade and handle
	spray bottle
	cooling rack

CHOCOLATE PEANUT BUTTER

You're gonna laugh when you find out what makes these so good. Are you ready? No, I can't tell you—I'm a little embarrassed. Okay, okay, you promise you won't pick on me? Ya really, really promise? Chocolate peanut butter cups! Yup, it's that simple, folks. I ain't above putting something delicious that someone else made into something I'm making. I like to think I'm just obeying Occam's Razor, ya know? Or something like that. . . .

Aside from the addition of chocolate peanut butter cups (and the shaping, of course), everything in this recipe is very similar to the free-form hearth sourdough loaf (Lesson 6).

1. Gather your foodstuff and tools.

2. Make your sourdough pre-ferment. Use starter that is sour smelling in a good way, most likely between 12 and 24 hours old. Make your pre-ferment 8 to

12 hours before you want to start mixing your dough—likely in the evening before you go to bed or in the morning. You want it to be the consistency of thick pancake batter. Put this stuff in a big bowl:

	12 POCKET-BREADS	24 POCKET-BREADS	48 POCKET-BREADS
sourdough starter	1 Tbsp/ 15 g	2 Tbsp/ 30 g	¼ cup/ 60 g
cool water (60°F/15°C)	½ cup/ 120 g	1 cup/ 240 g	2 cups/ 480 g
whole-wheat flour	¾ cup/ 105 g	1½ cups/ 210 g	3 cups/ 420 g

Mix it up real good. Cover with a plate or plastic wrap and leave it alone for 8 to 12 hours.

3. Chop your peanut butter cups. Here's your chance to use your favorite type of peanut butter cups. Don't act like you don't have a fave. Just chop them up into roughly ¼-in/6-mm pieces:

	12 POCKET-BREADS	24 POCKET-BREADS	48 POCKET-BREADS
chocolate peanut butter cups, chopped	1 cup/ 220 g	2 cups/ 440 g	4 cups/ 880 g

4. Mix the dough. Uncover the bowl of sourdough pre-ferment, and take a big whiff. It should be putting off a pretty strong smell, nice and yummy, maybe a touch sour. Add:

Chop 'em up.

	12 POCKET-BREADS	24 POCKET-BREADS	48 POCKET-BREADS
lukewarm water (80°F/27°C)	1¼ cups/ 300 g	2½ cups/ 600 g	5 cups/ 1,200 g
bread flour	3 cups/ 450 g	6 cups/ 900 g	12 cups/ 1,800 g
sea salt, fine grind	2 tsp/ 12 g	4 tsp/ 24 g	2 Tbsp plus 2 tsp/ 48 g
chocolate peanut butter cups	all of them	all of them	all of them

Mix everything together so that it's evenly combined, just for 30 seconds to a minute. Cover with a plate or plastic wrap, and let it sit for 30 minutes to an hour, whatever is convenient.

Mush 'em in there!

Plop 'em in the tin.

5. Gently stretch and fold the dough. Dip your hand in a bowl of water, then reach down into the side of the dough bowl, grab a little bit of it, and pull it up and push it down on top of the dough. Rotate the bowl a little bit and do it again to another portion of the dough. Give the dough about ten stretches and folds. Cover the dough, and let it sit for ½ hour.

6. Stretch and fold a few more times. After ½ hour, stretch and fold the dough another ten times. Cover the dough, and leave it alone for another ½ hour or so. Do this another two times, at 15- to 30-minute intervals.

7. Choose your own path. Choose your own adventure for the **bulk rise.**

If you want to shape your pocketbreads in 3 to 4 hours, let the dough sit out somewhere in your kitchen.

If you want to shape your pocketbreads anywhere from 12 to 48 hours later, stick it in the fridge (or just outside if it's cool out—about 45°F/7°C).

8. Grease your muffin tin. Use vegetable oil or nonstick spray to coat the individual cups.

9. Shape your pocketbreads. Flour your counter and dump out the dough. Cut the dough into ¾-cup/100-g pieces (to fill up your muffin tin about two-thirds of the way) and use a little bit of flour on your hands to shape them into round balls. Plop the pocketbreads into your muffin tin, seam-side down. When you're all done, put the whole thing in a plastic bag, so that the tops don't dry out. (A CLEAN garbage bag works great.)

10. Choose your own path. Choose your own adventure for the **final rise.**

If you want to bake your pocketbreads in 3 to 4 hours, let them sit out somewhere in your kitchen.

If you want to bake them anywhere from 6 to 24 hours later, stick them in the fridge (or just outside if it's cool out—about 45°F/7°C).

11. Preheat. Once your pocketbreads have risen, preheat your oven to 450°F/230°C for 20 minutes. If you put the pocketbreads in the fridge, take them out while the oven is preheating so that they can warm up to room temperature before you bake them.

12. Bake your pocketbreads. Take the pans out of the plastic bag, slash the top of each pocketbread with a razor, spray their tops with water, using a spray bottle, and get them in the oven. Bake for 5 minutes, then quickly open the oven, spray them again, and just as quickly close the oven. Bake for another 25 minutes, and check on them. You'll know they are done when the slashed portions are good and dark brown.

13. Take the breads out of the pan, and let them cool on a cooling rack.

a million pocketbreads in one

Don't stop there! You can add whatever the heck you want to these yummy little treats. Here are a few more ideas—just follow the previous pocketbread recipe, swapping out the add-ins. And then try some of your own, and drop me a note to share how creative you've gotten.

cinnamon date

This was another "wandering around the co-op" revelation. I was meandering through the store, pondering what I could put in these small treats, when I stumbled across little date pieces that had been rolled in oat flour. Aside from being delicious, they were already the perfect-size chunks, meaning that I could use them without having to chop them up first. That sounded good to me! I added the cinnamon when I noticed the cinnamon-date combo in a favorite bread of mine.

Make a date soaker. Mix the following after you make your pre-ferment, so that the date pieces can get rehydrated before you mix them into your dough.

	12 POCKET-BREADS	24 POCKET-BREADS	48 POCKET-BREADS
date pieces	½ cup/ 90 g	1 cup/ 180 g	2 cups/ 360 g
hot water (100°F/ 38°C)	1 cup/ 240 g	2 cup/ 480 g	4 cups/ 960 g

When mixing up your final dough, add cinnamon and your drained soaker.

	12 POCKET-BREADS	24 POCKET-BREADS	48 POCKET-BREADS
cinnamon, ground	2 tsp	1 Tbsp plus 1 tsp	2 Tbsp plus 2 tsp
date soaker, drained	all of it	all of it	all of it

Follow the rest of the procedure for kneading, shaping, and baking your pocketbreads on page 173.

B(L)T

This ingenious pocketbread is the brainchild of Karen from Mission Pie. She got her hands on some killer sun-dried tomatoes from a local farm and excitedly handed them over one day, suggesting that I toss them into some pocketbreads along with some bacon. The resulting pocketbread was an almost ready-made BLT—the only thing you're missing is the lettuce. So bake these puppies up, then slice them in half and squish in some lettuce. And maybe some mayonnaise, salt, and pepper, too.

Cook the bacon. Line a baking sheet with foil and bake the slices in a 350°F/180°C oven for 10 to 12 minutes. Or fry it up in a pan, whatever you prefer. Then crumble it up.

	12 POCKET-BREADS	24 POCKET-BREADS	48 POCKET-BREADS
thick-cut bacon	4 slices/ 90 g	8 slices/ 180 g	16 slices/ 360 g

Make a sun-dried tomato soaker. Use kitchen shears or scissors to cut up the tomatoes into small pieces, then get them a-soakin'.

	12 POCKET-BREADS	24 POCKET-BREADS	48 POCKET-BREADS
sun-dried tomatoes, chopped	¼ cup/ 45 g	½ cup/ 90 g	1 cup/ 180 g
hot water (100°F/ 38°C)	½ cup/ 120 g	1 cup/ 240 g	2 cups/ 480 g

Follow the rest of the procedure for kneading, shaping, and baking your pocketbreads on page 173.

fig fennel

This is another delicious combination that I picked up from Dave Miller. He makes an incredible loaf that also includes walnuts, but the fig-fennel one-two punch is enough to make this one of my favorite pocketbreads of all time. Just coarsely chop the figs and let them soak overnight in a soaker, and grind the fennel seeds right before adding to your dough. Then make those pocketbreads and have a party.

Make a fig soaker. Mix the following after you mix up your pre-ferment, so that the figs can get rehydrated before you mix them into your dough.

	12 POCKET-BREADS	24 POCKET-BREADS	48 POCKET-BREADS
dried figs, coarsely chopped	½ cup/ 90 g	1 cup/ 180 g	2 cups/ 360 g
hot water (100°F/ 38°C)	1 cup/ 240 g	2 cups/ 480 g	4 cups/ 960 g

When mixing up your final dough, add fennel seeds and your drained soaker. Grind the seeds right before adding them to your dough, and you'll unlock all of the flavor right into your pocketbreads.

	12 POCKET-BREADS	24 POCKET-BREADS	48 POCKET-BREADS
fennel seeds, ground	2 tsp	1 Tbsp plus 1 tsp	2 Tbsp plus 2 tsp
fig soaker, drained	all of it	all of it	all of it

Follow the rest of the procedure for kneading, shaping, and baking your pocketbreads on page 173.

cheddar chive

I like to use a nice sharp Cheddar for these guys. My favorite is made by the fine folk at Cabot Creamery, in my home state of Vermont. Just dice it into ¼- to ½-in/ 6- to 12-mm chunks. As for the chives, go for fresh if you've got 'em, though dried will work in a pinch.

	12 POCKET-BREADS	24 POCKET-BREADS	48 POCKET-BREADS
Cheddar cheese, diced	½ cup/ 200 g	1 cup/ 400 g	2 cups/ 800 g
chives, chopped finely	1 Tbsp fresh or 1 tsp dried	2 Tbsp fresh or 2 tsp dried	¼ cup fresh or 4 tsp dried

Follow the rest of the procedure for kneading, shaping, and baking your pocketbreads on page 173.

yum, cheddar-y goodness!

CHAPTER 8

I'M OPENING A BAKERY!?!?! / SWEET TREATS

Back at Mission Pie, things were going great one day a week, so I asked Karen and Krystin if we could bump it up to two days a week. Of course, they generously obliged. And people just kept buying the bread! When I first started baking there, I was buying all of my flour myself—driving up to Petaluma (an hour north of San Francisco) and filling up my car with 600 pounds at a time—and storing it in my bedroom. One day I inquired, "Maybe I could get my flour delivered right to the bakery?" Again, they said yes.

And this is the way it went for the next year:

"Is it okay to leave my dough in the fridge overnight?"

"Do ya mind if I use your scale?"

"Can I invite someone else in to help me shape loaves?"

"Could I bake a little earlier in the day?"

"Would you mind helping me carry this 100-pound rack up the stairs?"

They always said yes. And because of their amazing support, the business just kept growing and growing and growing. I started out baking 35 or 40 loaves one day a week, and it just steadily increased, until at the end of my time there I was baking 140 loaves a day twice a week. It was awesome, and I honestly couldn't believe it was happening.

Then one day I got an e-mail out of the blue from Jeremy Tooker, a buddy who owned an amazing café and coffee roastery in San Francisco, FourBarrel Coffee:

"Hey Josey—
I was wondering if you have some time to chat about business stuff soon. I have an idea and a space that we could work on together if you're interested.
Jeremy"

IF I WAS INTERESTED?!?
Uhh, jeez, let me think about that. Ummmmmmm . . . Hell yes I am interested, Jeremy goddamn Tooker, I am very frikkin' interested.

He wanted to open another café in another part of town, and he wanted me to have a bakery in it. He'd just found a great space, and in talking with folks who lived in that neighborhood, he learned that everybody wanted a bakery. So did I want to move in with him and his coffee business, and take this breadventure all the way?

Fast forward a year and a half, and we've opened The Mill. It's a café bakery—Jeremy and his crew manage the café, I manage the bakery. Why is it called "The Mill"? Because I've got a stone mill in the bakery that I use to mill all of our whole-grain flours.

This all sounds great, right? I know! But wait a second—at the time, I only really knew how to bake bread. I decided I'd better learn how to bake a bunch of coffeeshop treats right quick. So I started doing the same thing with a bunch of other baked goods that I did with bread—reading about them as much I could, talking about them as much as I could, and, most important, actually making them as much as I could.

My first experiments were pretty pathetic. I figured that I was a pretty good bread baker, able to riff on recipes, add my own flair, just basically follow my intuition. But holy moly—I learned very quickly that I had a lot to learn about all other baked goods. Perhaps my most humbling experience was the first time I tried my hand at a whole-wheat banana bread. I cobbled together several different recipes, taking the bits and pieces that I liked from each. What happened? It was the most ugly and disgusting banana bread the world has ever known. I literally threw the entire thing out before anybody could see it, let alone taste it. (It was raw and somehow a shade of pink on the inside, if you really must know. Please don't tell anybody; it's embarrassing.) Enter superbaker Wendy Thomas, a woman whose baking skills were surpassed only by her Viking strength. Wendy helped create and refine all of the recipes in this chapter, and I'm eternally grateful for her.

I've come a long way since then, and these recipes are the fruits of that labor.

WHAT YOU'LL NEED

FOODSTUFF	TOOLS
unsalted butter	frying pan, preferably one with a light-colored cooking surface
white sugar	sharp knife
dark brown sugar	big mixing bowl
sea salt, fine and coarse grind	measuring cups
vanilla extract	measuring spoons
eggs	whisk
all-purpose flour	mixing spoon
baking soda	baking sheet
semisweet chocolate, bar and chips or chunks	nonstick spray or parchment paper
	spatula
	cooling rack

There are many possible additions! See Other Delicious Cookies, page 196, for suggestions.

CHOCOLATE CHIP COOKIES

One day when I was home in Vermont hanging with my mom, she suggested I try a chocolate chip cookie recipe from *Cook's Illustrated*, and, my god, it blew me away. Cookies aren't the most difficult thing to bake, but these were jaw-droppingly delicious the very first time. I tweaked a few things here and there to suit my taste, and I hope you like the results. When I first made them I tossed in chocolate chips, but then I figured, why not try throwing in some other stuff and see what happens? What happened? I learned that this recipe is the base for a whole bunch of other cookies, and that making different types of cookies doesn't have to be very hard at all. There are two ways you can screw up this recipe: (1) overmixing the dough, and (2) overbaking the cookies. So be impatient at these two phases. They're going to look underbaked, especially in the middle. But trust me. I mean, raw cookie dough is delicious anyway, right?

1. Gather your foodstuff and tools.

2. Brown that butter. Put the butter in a frying pan (preferably a light-colored one, so you can see the color change when the butter starts to turn brown), and cook over medium-high heat for a few minutes.

unsalted butter, cut into roughly ½-in/ 12-mm slices	14 Tbsp/200 g

Watch very closely, stirring and smelling the butter along the way. As the butter warms up, it'll start to boil. This is good—let it boil, and stir it. After 3 to 5 minutes of this, it will all of the sudden start giving off the aroma of toffee or butterscotch, and will turn brown. REMOVE IT FROM THE HEAT IMMEDIATELY, and pour it into a big mixing bowl. It's really easy to go from brown butter to black butter, so be swift here, baker.

⤷ A very good question!

WHAT IS HAPPENING WHEN I "BROWN" BUTTER?
The process of browning butter is marvelous. I mean, you take something that is already one of the most delicious things known to humanity, and you make it even better. It's too good to be true, really. Anyway, you're just evaporating water from the butter, then cooking the milk solids and turning them into gold. Okay, not gold, but almost.

3. Mix in some of the ingredients. Toss the following in with the butter:

White sugar	½ cup/100 g
Dark brown sugar	¾ cup, firmly packed/150 g
Sea salt, fine grind	1¼ tsp
Vanilla extract	2 tsp
Large egg yolk	1
Large egg	1

Use a whisk to mix for 2 minutes, until everything is fully mixed together.

4. Fold in the rest of the ingredients. Dump in this stuff first:

all-purpose flour	2 cups/255 g
baking soda	½ tsp

Mix until you just have a few streaks of flour, then pour in:

semisweet chocolate, chopped up	¾ cup/135 g
semisweet chocolate chips or chunks	¾ cup/135 g

Use a big spoon to fold it all together; another 5 seconds or so should do. Don't overmix the dough, baker! Get everything mixed, then put down that spoon!

⤷ A very good question!

WHY ARE YOU BEING SO UPTIGHT ABOUT HOW MUCH I MIX THIS COOKIE DOUGH?
I know, right? I'm usually not so uptight about stuff, but this is one of those places where a very natural tendency will lead you to be less than the best baker you can be. The short answer: If you overmix your cookie dough, your cookies will come out rubbery. The longer answer: You want to develop as little gluten as possible in your cookies, and mixing is what leads to gluten development. Remember all that amazing bread you baked? Well, in bread you *want* to develop gluten, because it helps your bread dough trap gas, thereby becoming nice and light and fluffy and a real pleasure to eat. But cookies are different—gluten will make them tough and rubbery, and nobody wants that, now do they?

5. Shape cookie balls. Use your hands to make little golf ball–size cookie balls (70 to 80 g is what I prefer) and put them on a plate. Do this with all of your cookie dough (minus the part that you eat). Sprinkle the tops with some nice coarse sea salt and put those cookie balls in the fridge for at least a day. (I've actually left unbaked cookie dough in the fridge for weeks, taking it out to bake or just eat raw when I feel like it. This may or may not be hazardous to your health, given the raw eggs, so you didn't hear it from me.)

➢ A very good question!

WHAT'LL HAPPEN IF I CHILL THE DOUGH?

Aw, come on, try it and see! You can wait a day, can't ya? It's not a huge deal, but it will most definitely improve the shape, texture, and color of the cookies, in my humble opinion. But the cookies will still be absolutely incredible, even if you bake them immediately after mixing. If you're feeling experimental, do a taste test: Bake half of the cookies right away, and put the other half in the fridge to bake off tomorrow. Then you can see for yourself and decide if the chill is worth the wait.

——————————

6. Preheat your oven. Put a rack in the middle, and turn the oven up to 375°F/190°C, and take those cookies out of the fridge so they can warm up. Let the oven preheat, and let your cookie dough warm up for about 20 minutes before baking.

7. Arrange the cookies on the sheet. Lightly coat your baking sheet with nonstick spray, or line it with parchment paper. Arrange the cookies on the sheet, with at least 2 in/5 cm of room on all sides. It's a bummer when the cookies spread into each other upon making this glorious transformation.

8. Bake those delicious little beauties. Okay, I'm about to be uptight again—DON'T OVERBAKE THESE COOKIES! I can't tell you exactly how long to bake them, because I'm not calibrated with your oven, but I can tell you this: **You should probably take the cookies out before you think they're done.** If you bake them too long, they will be good cookies, but they won't be the jaw-dropping cookies I want you to make. This will take somewhere between 8 and 12 minutes, depending on your oven. Check them at 8 minutes just to be sure, but they will probably need another 2 to 4 minutes. You'll know they're done when they're a beautiful light brown; the middles will still look a little gooey, but the outsides will push back ever so slightly when you poke them with your finger. Take them out when you say, "Ehhh, I think they need another couple of minutes."

9. Let cool for a couple of minutes, then transfer to a cooling rack. Let them cool on the baking sheet for at least 5 minutes, then use a spatula to transfer them to a cooling rack. Or just eat them. These cookies are going to be awesomely gooey, so don't be impatient here or they'll just fall apart on you. And please share your delicious cookies, ya hear?

other delicious cookies

You can make a bunch of different cookies by following the exact same procedure as for the chocolate chip cookies! Totally awesome, right? Just substitute the stuff given here for the ingredients in step 4 of Chocolate Chip Cookies, page 194.

oatmeal raisin

all-purpose flour	1 cup/125 g
rolled oats	1¼ cups/130 g
raisins	¾ cup/120 g
baking soda	½ tsp
cinnamon, ground	1 tsp
nutmeg, ground	½ tsp

pecan

all-purpose flour	2 cups/255 g
baking soda	½ tsp
pecans, toasted and coarsely chopped (see page 114)	1 cup/120 g

walnut

all-purpose flour	2 cups/255 g
baking soda	½ tsp
walnuts, toasted and coarsely chopped (see page 114)	1 cup/120 g
cinnamon, ground	1 tsp

peanut butter

all-purpose flour	2¼ cups/285 g
baking soda	½ tsp
chunky peanut butter	¾ cup/200 g

WHAT YOU'LL NEED

FOODSTUFF	TOOLS
all-purpose flour	measuring cups
whole-wheat pastry flour	measuring spoons
white sugar	big mixing bowl
baking powder	mixing spoon
sea salt, fine grind	knife or pastry cutter
unsalted butter	spatula or bench knife
filling ingredients (see page 201; optional)	nonstick spray or parchment paper
heavy cream	baking sheet
crème fraîche (optional)	cooling rack

CREAM SCONES

Most scones suck. Why do they suck? Because they're dry as hell. Don't act like you don't know what I'm talking about! When was the last time you had a scone and didn't say, "I don't know, this is just a little dry for me." Or maybe you haven't even had a scone in a long time, because the last one you ate was so crappy. Anyway, it's not hard to make scones that are moist and delicious. And once you get the basic scone recipe down, you can riff on it all you want, adding fruit, spices and herbs, cheese, whatever. This recipe is for a "cream scone," which in my humble opinion is the best type. Some scones just have milk and egg in them, others have buttermilk, but these omit all of that stuff for über-delicious and fatty cream. Are they healthful? No, they are not. But what the hell, exercise feels good, so eat as many as you want and then go ride your bike, baker.

1. Gather your foodstuff and tools.

2. Mix the dry ingredients. Mix together in a big bowl:

all-purpose flour	1 cup/125 g
whole-wheat pastry flour	1 cup/100 g
white sugar	¼ cup/50 g (use 2 Tbsp if making savory scones)
baking powder	1 Tbsp
sea salt, fine grind	¼ tsp

3. Cut up the butter into tiny pieces. Use a knife or pastry cutter to chop the butter up into small cubes, no more than ¼ in/6 mm:

unsalted butter	12 Tbsp/170 g

Dump this into the bowl of dry ingredients, and put the whole bowl in the fridge for ½ hour. You want everything to be nice and cold before you do the next step, so don't rush it.

↘ A very good question!

WHY DO I NEED EVERYTHING TO BE COLD FOR MY SCONES?

Scones have a lot of butter in them. The tricky thing with this is that your hands are very warm compared to the butter, and they will make it melt. You don't want that; you want the butter to stay cool and solid throughout the whole process, right up until it goes into the oven and performs its magic. So don't skimp on me here, baker; put it in the fridge.

---

4. Preheat your oven. Take all that excitement and use it to put a rack in the middle of your oven and preheat to 375°F/190°C for about 30 minutes. Then read a book or maybe just sit and ponder life until all that stuff is nice and cold and your oven is nice and hot.

5. Cut in the butter. Take that cold bowl out of the fridge, and cut the butter into the flour with a spatula, bench knife, pastry cutter, or your fingers if you must, breaking it up into small pieces. You want all of the butter to be no bigger than peas, and most of it more like coarse sand.

6. Fold in the filling ingredients of your choice. Toss in the special stuff and mix 'til everything's dispersed evenly.

7. Mix in the cream. Now pour in that delicious, magical liquid known as heavy cream, and mush it up with your hands:

heavy cream   **1 cup/240 ml**

Optional bonus move: Replace ⅓ cup/75 ml of the heavy cream with crème fraîche. WHOA.

This dough should feel pretty darn stiff, very similar to playdough. Once all the cream is absorbed, turn the dough out onto a floured counter and fold the dough over on itself repeatedly for about 30 seconds. Not too much, just enough to give it the strength to stand up in the oven.

8. Gently shape the scones. Use nonstick spray or put a piece of parchment paper on your baking sheet. Gently grab about ¼ cup/100 g of scone dough, and lightly form it into a ball. Place each scone on your baking sheet, with about 3 in/7.5 cm of space around each one. They are going to spread out, so don't crowd these suckers! If you're doing sweet scones, brush their tops with cream and sprinkle with sugar.

9. Bake those babies off. Into the oven! Take care not to overbake these little sweeties. Set your timer for 10 minutes and take a peek, but likely they'll need another 8 to 12 minutes. You'll know they're done when their peaks and perimeters are starting to turn dark brown.

10. Once they're done, take them out and let them cool on the baking sheet for 5 minutes, then use a spatula or bench knife to move them to a cooling rack. Let them cool for 5 minutes, then eat them all and take a nap.

cheddar + sausage + onions = so tasty!

other delicious cream scones

There are endless options, but for sweet scones I like to pick a fruit (or two or three) that's in season, and let it speak loudly. The savory scones I suggest are much less reliant on fresh produce, so pick one of those if you're not feeling seasonal. These are just suggestions; feel free to follow your heart on this one. Regardless of which variation you choose, the rest of the recipe is exactly the same. Just fold in the stuff of your choosing in step 6 of the basic recipe (see page 198).

spring: corn cherry

fresh corn kernels	1/2 cup/75 g
dried cherries	1/2 cup/90 g
cornmeal	1/4 cup/40 g (replaces an equal amount of all-purpose flour)

summer: strawberry

strawberries, coarsely chopped, then frozen	1 cup/150 g

fall: apple cinnamon

tart apples, coarsely chopped	1 cup/110 g
cinnamon, ground	1 tsp
nutmeg, ground	1/2 tsp

winter: lemon ginger

crystallized ginger, chopped	1/4 cup/40 g
ginger, ground	1 tsp
lemon zest	1/2 tsp

winter: maple walnut

walnuts, toasted and coarsely chopped (see page 114)	1 cup/120 g

Once they're baked, brush their tops with a hearty slop of **maple syrup**—1/4 **cup/60 ml** should be enough for a batch. Special thanks to Karen and Krystin at Mission Pie for this one.

If you're after a savory scone, try one of these puppies. Just cut down on the sugar when you're making the scone dough—add only half of the usual amount.

gruyère

Gruyère cheese, grated	1 cup/130 g
black pepper, freshly ground	1 tsp
fresh thyme	1 tsp

sausage

sausage, cooked, coarsely chopped	½ cup/115 g
Cheddar cheese, grated	¼ cup/35 g
green onions, finely chopped	2 Tbsp

spicy corn

corn kernels, fresh	½ cup/75 g
cornmeal	¼ cup/40 g (replaces an equal amount of all-purpose flour)
red pepper flakes	2 tsp

olive

kalamata olives, pitted and coarsely chopped	½ cup/70 g
lemon zest	½ tsp
fresh rosemary, finely chopped	1 tsp

WHAT YOU'LL NEED

FOODSTUFF	TOOLS
filling ingredients (see page 206)	knife
unsalted butter	baking dish (12 by 8 by 3 in/31 by 20 by 7 cm or equivalent)
all-purpose flour	frying pan
white sugar	measuring cups
dark brown sugar	measuring spoons
pecans OR almonds OR walnuts	small mixing bowl
sea salt, fine grind	mixing spoon
ice cream	

SEASONAL FRUIT CRUMBLE

My friend Samin would most definitely disagree with me, but crumbles are so easy to make they're stupid. All you do is cover some delicious fruit with a crumble of nuts, sugar, butter, and maybe a little flour, then toss it in the oven for 45 minutes. I give you a handful of suggestions for fillings, organized by season. These are just meant to inspire, so please don't feel limited by them. If you've never made one, you're going to be really proud of yourself after this, because you just cannot mess it up. Well, that's not totally true. If you do mess it up, quickly discard it and tell everybody that the dog ate it. Then write to me personally; I will coach you through it.

1. Gather your foodstuff and tools.

2. Preheat the oven. Set it to 375°F/190°C and get to work.

3. Prepare your filling. The preparations here are very simple, folks. Chop up your fruit, mix it with the other filling ingredients, and pour it into a buttered baking dish.

4. Melt the butter. Put butter in a frying pan and cook over medium heat for a couple of minutes, just until it's melted:

unsalted butter, cut into 5 or 6 chunks	½ cup/115 g

5. Mix the rest of the ingredients for the crumble topping. Mix in a bowl while your butter melts:

all-purpose flour	1 cup/150 g
white sugar	¼ cup/50 g
dark brown sugar	¼ cup, firmly packed/50 g
pecans, almonds, or walnuts, toasted and coarsely chopped (see page 114)	1 cup/120 g
sea salt, fine grind	½ tsp

6. Mix in the butter. Once the butter's all melted, take it off the heat and let it cool down for a few minutes. Then dump it right in with your dry ingredients and stir it all up.

7. Sprinkle the crumble, and get that sucker in the oven. Evenly sprinkle your freshly made crumble topping atop your prepared fruit filling. Now shove it in the oven! Bake for 35 to 45 minutes, 'til the juices are bubbling and the crumble is golden brown and the whole kitchen smells delicious.

8. Let it cool for 20 minutes, then eat it with some ice cream, and send me an e-mail telling me how much you love life.

a million crumbles in one

Of course, there are endless options. Just pick a fruit (or two or three) that's in season, and make it happen. These are just the tip of the iceberg—don't be scared to follow your intuition here, baker. Regardless of which fruit you pick, the rest of the recipe doesn't change.

spring: cherry

It sure is a pain to pit all these cherries, but ya know, progress rarely comes without struggle by its side.

fresh sour cherries, pitted	6 cups/790 g
white sugar	1 cup/200 g
cornstarch	1 Tbsp
sea salt, fine grind	1/2 tsp

summer: strawberry rhubarb

I have a severe sweet tooth, so I really wanted to just make this a strawberry crumble. I tried it out (and it was very, very delicious), but I realized that the tartness of rhubarb really is the perfect complement to the sinfully delicious sweetness of ripe strawberries.

strawberries, halved	3 cups/450 g
rhubarb, cut into 1/2-in/ 12-mm chunks	3 cups/360 g
white sugar	1/2 cup/100 g
cornstarch	1 Tbsp
sea salt, fine grind	1/2 tsp
lemon juice	1 lemon's worth, more or less

summer: peach

There really isn't much that's better than a peach at its peak. Except maybe a peach at its peak in this crumble! If you've got a nasty hankering for this in the middle of winter, you could go with frozen, but you didn't hear that from me.

peaches, cut into 1/2-in/ 12-mm slices	7 or 8 big ones
white sugar	1/4 cup/50 g
sea salt, fine grind	1/2 tsp
lemon juice	1 lemon's worth, more or less

fall: apple cranberry

This one's best in the fall, but in truth you can get yummy apples almost any time of year. I like to use a tart variety, such as Cortland or Granny Smith.

apples, cut into $\frac{1}{2}$-in/ 12-mm slices	5 or 6 big ones
cranberries, dried	1 cup/160 g
white sugar	$\frac{1}{2}$ cup/100 g
cinnamon, ground	1 tsp
nutmeg, ground	$\frac{1}{2}$ tsp
sea salt, fine grind	$\frac{1}{2}$ tsp
lemon juice	1 lemon's worth, more or less

winter: ginger pear

You can omit the ginger if you're a weenie, but its sharpness really does wonders to balance out the mellow pear.

pears, cut into $\frac{1}{2}$-in/ 12-mm slices	7 or 8 big ones
white sugar	$\frac{1}{2}$ cup/100 g
crystallized ginger, chopped	$\frac{1}{2}$ cup/80 g
sea salt, fine grind	$\frac{1}{2}$ tsp
lemon juice	1 lemon's worth, more or less

FOODSTUFF	TOOLS
cornmeal	measuring cups
buttermilk	2 small mixing bowls
Kamut flour	mixing spoon
baking powder	plastic wrap or plate (for covering small bowl)
baking soda	measuring spoons
sea salt, fine grind	big mixing bowl
unsalted butter	frying pan
honey	loaf pan (about 8 by 4 in/20 by 10 cm)
dark brown sugar	toothpick
egg	cooling rack

CORNBREAD

When I was deep in recipe development mode for The Mill, I was searching for a baked good that would really highlight freshly milled grains, but that I could also make year-round. I wanted something that I could see myself eating on the regular, something uncontroversial, unfussy, unassuming. I went looking through my old notebook for ideas and immediately came upon a potential solution: cornbread. Yes! Now I just had to figure out how to make it. I tried a ton of different recipes from any source I could find. I scoured the Internet, looked through all of my books, and had friends and family send me their favorite recipes. After many dishes, pans, and muffins, I began to cobble together my own version, a combination of my favorite pieces from all the recipes I tried. I was getting closer and closer, but then one day I remembered a recipe that my friend Bronwen had told me about years ago, the best cornbread she'd ever had. And luckily enough, it happened to be in one of the first bread books I'd ever gotten: Peter Reinhart's *Crust and Crumb*. Lo and behold, Peter had figured it out. I took his recipe as my base (which already incorporated almost all of the elements I'd discovered I loved, like an overnight buttermilk/cornmeal soaker) and tweaked it to fit my needs. The main difference between my recipe and his is that I use Kamut flour instead of all-purpose. Since Kamut flour soaks up more liquid than all-purpose flour (and has a totally delicious, sweet flavor), I had to make some adjustments, but the result is the most moist and sweet and delicious cornbread I've ever had. I hope you feel the same, baker.

If you don't have or can't get Kamut flour, you can substitute whole-wheat pastry flour. If you don't have any or don't want to do that, then substitute all-purpose flour. Just increase the flour quantity to 1¼ cups/190 g.

1. Make the cornmeal soaker. One night before you go to bed, mix this up in a small bowl:

cornmeal	³/₄ cup/120 g
buttermilk	1 cup/240 ml

Cover it and put it in the fridge overnight. The next day, take the soaker out of the fridge an hour before proceeding, and preheat the oven to 375°F/190°C.

2. Mix the dry ingredients. In a big mixing bowl, mix:

Kamut flour	1 cup/150 g
baking powder	1 Tbsp
baking soda	¹/₄ tsp
sea salt, fine grind	³/₄ tsp

3. Melt the butter. Toss into a frying pan over medium heat:

unsalted butter	3 Tbsp

4. Butter your pan. Pour half of the melted butter into the loaf pan, and tilt to cover the sides with butter.

5. Mix the honey and butter. Pour the following into the melted butter remaining in the frying pan, and stir so that it all melts together:

honey	1 Tbsp plus 1 tsp/25 g

6. Mix the rest of the ingredients. Mix the following into the cornmeal soaker:

dark brown sugar	¹/₄ cup, firmly packed/50 g
buttermilk	1 cup/240 ml
egg	1 extra large

7. Mix it all together. Add the soaker and the honey-butter mixture to the dry ingredients, and beat with a large spoon for about 60 seconds. Don't shortchange this, baker—Kamut flour requires some extra work in order to develop the strength it needs to make this cornbread stand up in the oven. It should be the consistency of thick pancake batter, so add 1 to 2 Tbsp of buttermilk if it's too thick, or 1 to 2 Tbsp of Kamut flour if it's too thin. Pour the batter into the prepared loaf pan.

8. Bake it. Get the pan into the preheated oven, and leave it alone for 30 minutes. Rotate the pan, and leave it for another 30 minutes, then do the ol' toothpick test: Insert a dry toothpick into the center to see if it comes out clean. If the inside's still wet, leave it in the oven for another 10 to 15 minutes, or until a toothpick comes out nice and clean.

9. Cool it. Let your cornbread cool in its pan for at least 5 minutes before turning it out onto a cooling rack. I like to serve this guy upside down, because it gets so gorgeous and dark brown on the bottom. But do whatever you wish!

WHAT YOU'LL NEED

FOODSTUFF	TOOLS
whole oat groats	quart/liter container and lid (yogurt tub or mason jar)
rolled oats (not "instant")	measuring cups
water	mixing spoon
raisins	cooking pot
walnuts	measuring spoons
maple syrup	cereal bowl
flaxseed oil	
sea salt, fine grind	

RAFI'S OVERNIGHT OATS

This is another recipe that has is its roots in my dearest bro and visionary Rafi. A few years back he got his hands on a copy of a book called *Nourishing Traditions*; and very soon after, the kitchen cupboards were filled with bubbling, stinky jars of many an unidentifiable substance. (This book is where Rafi got his idea for the "Pemmican Warrior Cleanse Adventure" I describe on page 98.) While many of these jars came and went, one of them stuck around: fermented oats. Every morning I'd watch Rafi pull the mason jar out of the cupboard and scoop a mound of stinky slop into a pot on the stovetop. Five minutes later he'd be devouring his feast. I was pretty grossed out by this affair one morning, and was expressing this sentiment to him, when he insisted that I try his concoction. Holy crap; it was incredible. By letting the oats soak for days at a time, Rafi was letting those magical little microorganisms (very similar to those found in your sourdough starter) do their thing, thereby creating an array of new nuanced flavors and aromas, not to mention the health benefits of the "predigestion" that

they were also accomplishing. About two days of fermenting led to the oats having a wonderfully sweet, lactic-acid-forward smell and taste, and after that they moved decidedly into the sour realm. But Rafi just adjusted the amount of maple syrup that he added upon cooking the oats accordingly and didn't worry about it.

1. Make the oat soaker. One day when you're feeling brave, mix up the following in a quart/liter container:

whole oat groats	1 cup/190 g
rolled oats	2 cups/210 g

Pour in enough water to cover the oats by about ½ in/ 12 mm:

cool water	about 2 cups/480 g

Cover your container and leave it alone for a day or two. At this point the soaking oats should have developed a nice, lightly fermented smell, which you can check by just taking a big whiff—it should smell faintly like yogurt. At this point I usually just put the oats in the fridge, where they can live until you're ready to cook up a batch. (Rafi likes to leave his oats in the cupboard for the whole week, and by the end of it the oats are *reallllly* sour.)

2. Cook those oats. Scoop out ½ to ¾ cup/100 to 140 g of the soaked oats into a pot, and then pour in an equal amount of cold water. Put it on the stovetop over high heat 'til they start to boil, then turn down the heat to a simmer. Meanwhile . . .

3. Prepare your bowl. While the oats are cooking, dump the following into your favorite cereal bowl:

raisins (whatever kind you like)	**¼ cup/45 g**
walnuts, toasted and coarsely chopped (see page 114)	**2 Tbsp**
maple syrup	**1 Tbsp**
flaxseed oil	**1 Tbsp**
sea salt, fine grind	**¼ tsp**

Let the oats cook for about 5 minutes, stirring along the way, until they've thickened into a delicious porridge.

4. Combine, mix, and enjoy. Once the oats are cooked, pour them into your prepared bowl, mix it all up, and say a little prayer for Rafi.

Of course, there are endless variations on this very simple breakfast. I like to add fresh bananas or apples on the regular, but add whatever fruit you like. Also, you can swap out the maple syrup for brown sugar, or honey, or agave nectar. A nice dollop of yogurt is a heavenly addition. Whatever you do, just please don't forget the salt.

THANK YOU

I've been lucky enough to cross paths with some real badasses. Thanks, you guys. I love you all so hard. You're the best.

my mom and dad—because you made me and loved me and always encouraged me to be myself (even when I was obsessed with Snoop Dogg in middle school)

my step-folks Ellen and Mike—because you raised me like I was your own (even through that whole Snoop Dogg thing)

Cathy—because you are without a doubt better than the best girl a boy could ever dream of, and I still can't believe I get to hang out with you every day

Rafi—because you almost never told me to stop talking about bread with you (even when you obviously really didn't give a damn)

Jed—because you are the best brother (and you finally forgave me for all that stuff from when we were kids)

Jeremy T—because you asked me to marry you on our first date (and showed me the joys of slapping)

Jodi—because you showed me the Path of the Kind Assassin (and you always called me bro)

Charlie H—because you showed me how generous a stranger can be (and for all the sleepovers—oh, those sleepovers)

Karen and Krystin—because you helped me carry that speed rack up the stairs (and oh, ya know, just frikkin' kick-started my business times a million, no big deal)

Rob S—because you reminded me that if I know how to do it better, I should just do it better (and that time you put my tie on your head like a warrior)

Roman H—because you transferred incalculable amounts of energy into The Mill (Splinter would be so, so proud of you)

Trevor M—because you taught me fierce Viking compassion (and how to tile)

Ian and Elicia—because you let me leave the tent when I started breaking stuff (and didn't pick on me when I was totally freaking out on toast bar)

Soupy Dave—because you fanned the flame (and let me touch your dough)

Blaire and Andrew—because you showed me how badass two bakers can be (and shared the joys of Heady Topper)

Brendan—because you were my pump-master when I first started covering the house in flour (and my best baguette critic)

Sarah B—because you walked in that day at Mission Pie and asked me to write this book

Adam from Bread & Butter—because you showed me the magic of rye

Chad R—because you gave me an ideal

Larry, Colter, and David—because you shared your sacred space

Monica Spiller—because you baked me your barm bread

Lawrence and Jeff—because you invited me into your restaurant the day we met (and taught me lots of dirty jokes [L] and cutting-edge fashion [J])

Brian—because you gave me the keys to your pizza place

Krup—because you let me stick my face in your smoky oven

Mr. Miller—because you showed me the way

Wendy—because you taught me how to run a bakery

Burl—because you stuck it out by my side, day after day, week after week, month after month, year after year

Ryan—because you said "hi" that day out front of 4B

Cobi—because you hit the ground running

whole
cranb
wa
$ 6.

INDEX